Jeremy Tankard Typography

Type book TWO

Introduction

This second volume, as with the first book, exists to show the typefaces designed by Jeremy Tankard. Due to its format and the space available, the more recent additions to the collection have been given greater prominence.

Aspect and The Shire Types have been extended to support most European languages. Aspect also benefits from two additional weights; ExtraBold and Heavy. The more recent typefaces include; the addition of Greek and Cyrillic scripts to the Bliss family, a serif type named Kingfisher and a sans serif, Wayfarer. As you can see from the contents page opposite, more typefaces and related information are available to view at www.typography.net.

The two texts included in this book have been written by Neil Macmillan and Jan Middendorp. In the first text, Neil reminisces on the years leading to the digital revolution in typesetting. In the second text, Jan discusses ideas that directly affect the practice of type design today. I am grateful to both Neil and Jan for their contributions.

Contents

The following typefaces are shown at www.typography.net

Alchemy	/type/alchemy.htm
Arjowiggins Inuit	/commissions/arjowiggins.htm
Blue Island	/type/blueisland.htm
Corbel	/type/corbel.htm
Disturbance	/type/disturbance.htm

Visit www.typography.net for additional information and samples of the typefaces shown in this book

How I became a man of many fonts

A personal reminiscence of typesetting in pre-PostScript times

NEIL MACMILLAN

Blessed with an affinity for letters of the alphabet since childhood my inability to achieve perfection in their reproduction was always a frustration. That didn't prevent me however from pursuing a career in which they played an enormous part. Working in commercial art and design was my goal. After 'Letrasetting' my way through several menial advertising jobs, joining the Edinburgh printing trade as an apprentice lithographic artist in the 1960s proved a real introduction to lettering, typefaces and typesetting.

At that time, in a city with a worldwide reputation for book production, most text type was still being set in metal. It was however a decade of change and a new generation of phototypesetting systems with faster, more reliable, electronically controlled machines was being introduced by the larger print companies to complement and eventually replace their hot metal (mostly Monotype) systems. My work at that time involved me with the more established display phototypesetting systems.

This was certainly the case when I returned to advertising some years later as a finished artist. In those days, lacking the hands-on WYSIWYG advantages of computer users today, designers and artists of the time had to 'spec' or 'mark-up' their copy for hot metal or photosetting which 'fingers crossed' would return from the typesetter as originally visualised. Help with this onerous task came in the form of type specimen books and leaflets which many typefounders, typesetters and printers distributed free of charge. Both Monotype and Linotype offered more sophisticated assistance with copyfitting tables which enabled much easier calculation. As I prepared my copy for typesetting little did I know how involved I was to become with typesetting and typefaces.

I bought my first font in the mid 1970s. And from then until the late 1980s I didn't really stop. Perhaps I should have said *we* bought *our* first font. My two partners and I were operating a successful finished art studio in Edinburgh servicing the city's advertising agencies, design companies, publishers and printers. As buying in typesetting from local suppliers was proving to be costly both in slowing down artwork turnround time and, more importantly, in depriving the company of a huge chunk of potential profitability, we decided to buy in our own kit. Compugraphic's Universal IV keyboard-operated direct-entry phototypesetter was our machine of choice. With a skilled typesetter on board we carefully chose a variety of fonts, in this case little strips of negative film, which would appeal to our more text-oriented customers.

Within the Compugraphic type library, which offered a reasonable choice for this purpose, many of the most popular trade typefaces had been redrawn and renamed. For example their version of Helvetica was Triumverate. This is a method of avoiding copyright infringement and expensive licensing agreements that's still prevalent today. Many of the fonts in the Compugraphic library had suffered the same fate. That, though, didn't deter our Compugraphic investment from 'bringing in the dosh' and providing the platform therefore for the future purchase of more sophisticated and expensive phototypesetting equipment. As demand for our Compugraphic type increased more and more fonts were purchased.

The major source of inspiration for this particularly enjoyable aspect of running a typesetting company was the quarterly publication *U&lc* issued by the International Typeface Corporation. ITC, a type manufacturing company founded in New York in 1970 by Aaron Burns, Herb Lubalin and Ed Rondthaler, offered both new designs and classic revivals most with notoriously exaggerated x-heights then much in demand by US advertising art directors. *U&lc*, as well as promoting ITC fonts, encouraged other manufacturers to use their publication to advertise the release of new typefaces.

My real aspiration at that time was to acquire one of Berthold's Diatype photolettering machines the output of which was considered the best ever by the typographic cognoscente. The Berlin typefounder H Berthold AG introduced the Diatype, its first typesetter, in 1958 and went on to sell over ten thousand of these trigger-operated

1

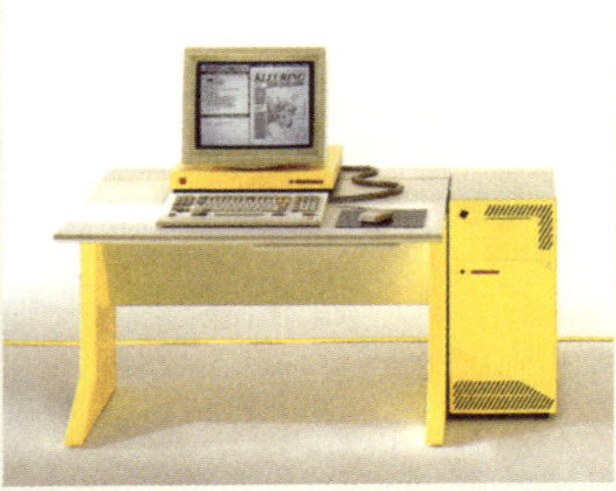

2

3

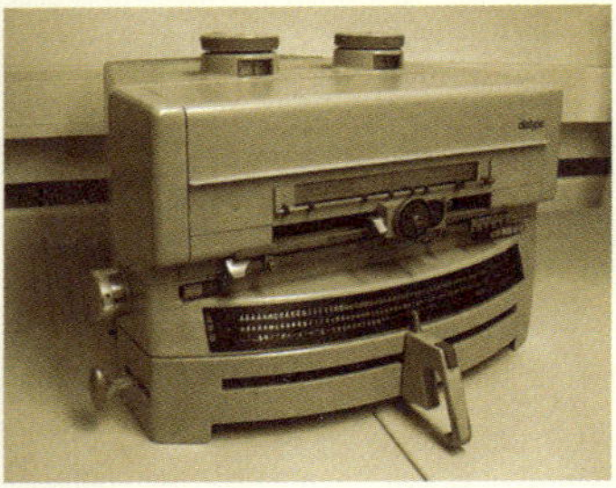

4

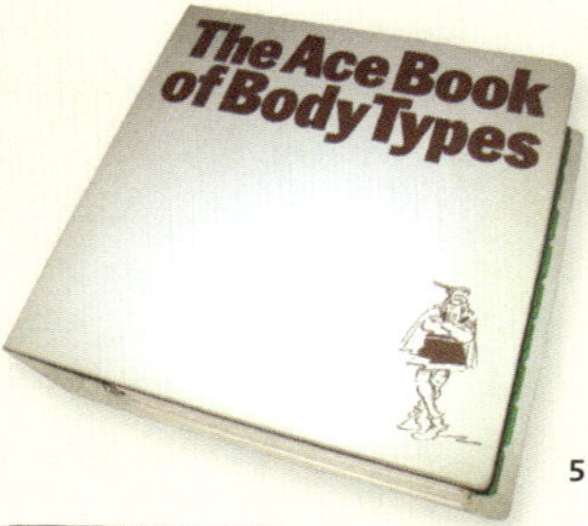
The Ace Book of Body Types

5

neo-Gill Sans
neo-Gill Sans
neo-Gill Sans
neo-Gill Sans
neo-Gill Sans
neo-Gill Sans
neo-Gill Sans
neo-Gill Sans
neo-Gill Sans

6

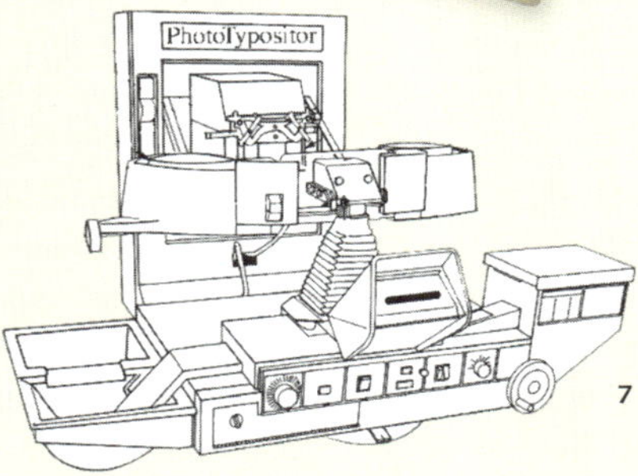
PhotoTypositor

7

machines. Although originally designed for the printed ephemera and cartographic markets the Diatype's single character exposure from precision manufactured glass font discs and carefully regulated inter-character spacing of the highest standard contributed to the desirability of its output for advertising work, particularly ad setting.

By the mid 1970s Berthold had streamlined the design of the Diatype but the second-hand model we eventually got our hands on had a general appearance eerily reminiscent of WWI German military hardware. This, however, did not impede the quality of output and armed with the most popular fonts of the moment we set about the advertising market with great enthusiasm. Our local art directors were influenced in their choice of typeface by their peers in the big London ad agencies who in turn were advised by their own typographers. The London market in the 1970s had produced a generation of type directors who influenced the world of advertising as never before. Such exponents of the craft as the late Maggie Lewis, Roger Kennedy, Dave Wakefield and Joe Hoza immediately spring to mind. Many from that era continue to influence typography in today's digital environment.

In order to attract customers to our Diatype body setting it became obvious that it was necessary to complement that service with a photoheadlining facility. The headlining market was dominated by one particular machine, the Visual Graphics Corporation's Phototypositor, a hand-cranked device, which exposed a character at a time through a film strip font, two inches wide by twelve feet long, on to light sensitive paper or film which was itself developed within the machine. A viewfinder enabled the operator to physically control the intercharacter spacing as each character appeared after exposure. VGC offered an enormous variety of two-inch film strip fonts from a

1 Gunter Gerhard Lange surveys the Edinburgh sky after opening the author's new office
2 The Berthold M Series Workstation
3 Georg Salden designing more fonts for his GST group
4 A 1970s Berthold Diatype
5 The author's company's type specimen book
6 The Neo-Headliners range of Gill Sans headlining fonts
7 The VGC Phototypositor

library which had developed from the 1960s under the the guidance of the aforementioned Aaron Burns.

Berthold's equivalent of VGC's 'Typositor', as it was commonly known, was the darkroom-operated Staromat. Limited by an alternative font format and unable therefore to take advantage of the huge availability of two-inch film strip fonts it proved much less popular. However its exclusive Berthold typefaces made it a 'must have' for typeshops seeking access to all available headline fonts.

As demand for high quality type increased my partners and I decided to spend big and replace our aging Diatypes with one of Berthold's keyboard-operated Diatronic machines. Launched by Berthold almost ten years earlier in 1967, the Diatronic achieved its quality by stationary exposure through one of its eight glass photomatrix grids. This resulted in even more fonts being purchased as the new acquisition meant, of course, that we had to at least duplicate our Diatype font library.

In the autumn of 1978 a designer friend working with Wolff Olins in London tipped me off about a sponsored trip to the Graphic Expo exhibition in New York which was being organised by Alphatype, an American manufacturer of typesetting systems. The aim was to encourage European typesetters to consider the Alphatype product, at that time the system of choice for the foremost American advertising typesetters. The trip proved a great success from a personal point of view. The new technology on show, particularly from Berthold, and the opportunity to meet with some of the leading members of the London typesetting fraternity gave me an insight into the future and led eventually to a break-up with my partners, the start of a new business, and considerably more spending on fonts.

The new company invested in Berthold's System 3000 which I'd seen in New York. It's floppy driven terminal, enabling jobs to be rerun and edited or corrected, interfaced with a photo-unit which, though utilising Diatronic font grids, offered an even higher quality of output and a considerably increased range of type sizes. Skilled operators, plus an additional investment in the more popular Berthold fonts and some of their exciting new releases, made for an immediate impact on the market which, though now highly competitive, was beginning to benefit from the 'eighties' boom in the UK economy.

The next ingredient that would ensure future success was a headlining capability. With a somewhat limited budget thanks to the Berthold spend, I bought an alternative more economic headlining machine manufactured by FotoStar International. An interesting fact about the proprietor of this California-based company, one Bob Trogman, was that it was he who designed the ubiquitous Blippo typeface, Handel Gothic and several other similar types which have benefitted from a recent 'seventies' revival. His FotoStar design combined elements of both the 'Typositor' and the Staromat and utilised two-inch film strip fonts.

With the FotoStar installed, the important process of building up the font library began. Aware, after my encounter with some of London's most prosperous advertising typesetters in New York, that attracting customers to your range of headlining fonts virtually guaranteed that you would be asked to supply the more lucrative body type, it was imperative that the library should be as comprehensive, and preferably as exclusive, as possible. To get up and running an initial font purchase from the vast library of the Visual Graphics Corporation, mostly of standard types, was supplemented by an miscellaneous selection which included several families from type designer Adrian Williams's company Fonts.

Meanwhile the search went on for exclusivity. Another type contact from my New York trip recommended an approach to the Typsettra company in Toronto. Established in 1968 by lettering artist and type designer Les Usherwood the company offered a font franchise of his exclusive designs. A short visit to Toronto sealed a deal and we became the first European company to offer Caxton and many more of Les's successful designs to our customers. The visit also revealed that Les and his company had cracked the method of manufacturing glass font grids for use on Berthold equipment. A real bonus as it enabled us to support their headline fonts with exclusive text setting.

Encouraged by the positive response of customers to the Typsettra library I continued to look out for similar opportunies. Some brilliant advertising in ITC's *U&lc* by a Scandinavian typesetting group Typografen AB drew my attention to the types of German designer Georg Salden. Salden had gathered together a group of

European typesetters, predominantly Berthold users, who paid him an annual fee for exclusive use of his types in their area. I soon became a member of GST, as the group was known, and much enjoyed their annual get-togethers where we approved Georg's new types and advised him on future direction. I remember particularly a meeting that took place in Bremen. It was my first of many encounters with Gunter Gerhard Lange, Berthold's artistic director, who was presenting one of his highly regarded 'Type Trends' talks. The ubiquitous Erik Spiekermann translated the talk from German for the English speakers who included myself, of course, and the late Ed Cleary. Those who know Erik and Herr Lange will be aware that together they are an irrepressible combination.

Without doubt the most impressive collection of headlining typefaces available for exclusive franchise was that of Headliners International of New York. Each family in their 'Neo' range of over 200 serif, sans-serif, and script typefaces was available in several weights, in some cases as many as ten, with outline and drop shadow versions. An advertising typographer's dream, I eventually secured the franchise for Scotland and although more of a rental than a purchase it did add almost two thousand two-inch film strip fonts to my tally.

It was Georg Salden who introduced me to the international organisation Association Typographique Internationale, founded by Charles Peignot in 1957 to provide a forum for those involved in all aspects of typography. I attended my first ATypI Annual Congress in 1988. Hosted by Linotype and held in the company's hometown of Frankfurt am Main, it was a prestigious affair offering a diverse programme of typographic presentations by leading lights of the Association. A particular highlight was my sharing of a lunch table with amongst others, Hermann Zapf, Adrian Frutiger and the brilliant Swiss typographer Max Caflisch. I also had the pleasure of meeting the late Aaron Burns.

Another highlight was an encounter with the illustrious Matthew Carter whilst waiting for our baggage at Heathrow after returning from Frankfurt. I'd introduced myself to Matthew and on discovering I ran a typesetting company he, by then a co-founder of Bitstream, asked if I planned to invest in PostScript fonts. My response was that I didn't at that time see a serious future for the Mac or PC, and at least my fonts were proprietorial and could not be copied by any Tom, Dick or Harry with access to a computer. Yes, I was disastrously wrong on the first point but certainly right about the threat to type design from copying – not much consolation now though.

By 1988 I'd already had a Mac on board for over three years – the Macintosh 512K which I bought with great expectation early in 1985. My initial excitement over its revolutionary abilities waned, however, as a result of its initial lack of usable software – there was no PostScript around then. Even after introducing my Mac to several designer friends as the future of the industry I'd decided that it would never be powerful enough to run real graphics applications and had proceeded to invest heavily in the new and exciting Berthold digital M Series.

This was seriously sexy kit, beautifully designed WYSIWYG Unix workstations driving a very high resolution image recorder running Berthold Diamond fonts, digital typefaces of the highest quality, which could be output at a razor-sharp maximum 240 millimetre cap height. Just thinking about it almost rekindles my love affair with all things Berthold. Needless to say it all came at a considerable price. The cost of the Diamond fonts alone, 1300 of them, was £75,000 – and even that was a special offer. (Some years later this all came back to haunt me when I worked on a promotion for a digital font retailer offering the Bitstream library of 1500 fonts for less than £1500.)

The end of the nineteen eighties saw the UK economy hit by recession, and with QuarkXPress, which had been introduced in 1987, along with a more powerful version of my old friend the Mac, making inroads into the studios of my biggest customers it became only too obvious that my font buying days were coming to an end. This did indeed prove to be the case. I took my company into voluntary liquidation in the September of 1991, its thirteenth year. Mine wasn't the first, and certainly not the last typesetting company, to suffer that ignominious fate.

But is it useful?

Random notes on the nature and culture of type design

JAN MIDDENDORP

The theatrics of type design

Design is about staging functions. I use the word 'staging' – *mettre en scène* in French, *inszenieren* in German – because the word captures several levels of 'putting it out there'. It implies making visible, but also making possible. On a theatre stage or in a film, a text or a set of ideas is brought to life and made visually interesting. Design is bringing to life and making visually interesting an act performed by an object. The extent to which that act – the object's function – depends on the design for it to happen at all may vary from object to object and from category to category. In some cases (say, a lamp) the function is carried out more or less independently from the design (in the lamp's case, by one or more light bulbs) and the design is wrapped around it, staging the function like a classical opera might be staged. We know what is going to happen but the effect lies in the way the performance is presented – the extent to which the setting enhances or obscures the familiar content, adding an element of surprise, making it more poignant or more intriguing. Conversely, in other instances, the design forms a unity with the function it helps to facilitate. This could be the case for certain toys, a corkscrew or a paperclip, for instance.

Graphic design and typography are not intrinsically at home at either end of the spectrum I just sketched. There is graphic design that is like window-dressing: the designer provides an attractive package – a 'skin' in interface design – to sell the contents. There is also graphic design that is inextricably interwoven with the designed object's function. This may be true where the main function is to be a visual statement, as with contemporary graphic design projects verging on art. But it also goes for many purely practical products, such as a functional calendar, signage system or website. I don't think that in any of these cases it is possible to recognize 'good' design by the immediacy, or inevitability, with which the form follows from the function. If part of the function is to communicate, then everybody has his or her own ideas (and every cultural niche its conventions and tastes) with regard to how to communicate best. If part of the design's theme is to show how the object works, e.g. by making visible the grid or the fixings, then appreciating that transparency ('form follows function' at it purest) is in itself a matter of culture, convention and taste.

*

So how does the staging of function work in type design? First of all, we must agree on what is 'form' and 'content' in type. Typefaces do not directly communicate or express language. The visual representation of language is the alphabet, a system of shapes that exists in our minds, independent (to a large extent, at least) of any specific typeface. The alphabet is a system of conventions that has taken thousands of years to evolve into its present state, but (in the case of the Latin alphabet) hasn't evolved that much during the past 500 years. The basic shapes of letters appear to be as unavoidably linked to their meaning as the shape of a bottle or a fork to their respective functions. We know this is not really true, because letters are purely conventional signs, but as the only function of an 'A' is to be recognized as 'A' (whatever sound it may represent), its shape has become as essential to its functioning as the teeth of a fork are to it being a fork.

Type design is conceiving forms to represent the alphabet. Because the basic function of a typeface is its faculty of being recognized, the designer needs to work within the conventions of his or her writing system. While in other design disciplines total originality may be a virtue – as long as a building or coffee machine performs its job, it is not necessarily a bad thing if it is not recognized as such at first sight – originality is obviously of limited use when designing type.

To get a better understanding of how a type designer moves, Roger Excoffon's analogy may come in handy. He famously likened the basic shape of the letter to a road on which type designers drive, each negotiating curves and avoiding obstacles in a different way –

particularities that add up to a person's individual style of driving. Of course, many type designers assume a different persona with each new typeface, although some – Gerard Unger and Adrian Frutiger come to mind – seem to have such a strong personality that their entire work is permeated by it. Each of their typefaces expresses roughly the same driving style.

Driving, acting, stage design... Do we really need all these analogies to make clear what type design is about? It seems we do. If there is any living type designer whose work should speak for itself, because of its no-frills functionality and sheer ubiquity, it is, again, Adrian Frutiger. Yet Frutiger's writings abound with analogies. He likens type design to fashion, dressing the naked; he argues that it responds to changing tastes much like car design does; spacing glyphs is like trees in a wood, etc. Each of theses analogies seems to have been conceived to convince an audience of outsiders that this kind of work makes sense in the greater scheme of things. Self-legitimation.

Type design and legitimation

In an age in which 'freedom', whatever it means, is often proclaimed to be the single most important criterion of human dignity and happiness, why would anyone with ample talents for visual organisation embrace the limitations of the letterform? In other words – what makes creative people choose type design as a career?

I recently interviewed Sara De Bondt, a young Belgian designer based in London. When taking the admission test for the St. Lukas College of Art and Design in Brussels at 18, De Bondt was still considering a career as a painter or sculptor. Parent pressure and coincidence led to her choosing the design department instead. She never looked back – and realised that design, not art, fits her personality best: 'I like working in response to a precise assignment. I would run into difficulties when starting from scratch, the way an artist does. It would be very hard for me to justify my choices... I would constantly question the legitimacy of my work.'

Legitimation is often an important aspect when it comes to career choices. It is not hard to imagine that for many talented imagemakers who choose design over 'fine art' (I actually prefer the Dutch term, which translates as 'free art') this decision was primarily driven by motives very similar to De Bondt's: a need for a decision process involving steps that are to some extent objective, verifiable and imposed by outside factors. To create, yes, but to create solutions, not simply expressions. Some of these instances have been documented. Shortly after the Bolshevist revolution in Russia, artists such as Rodchenko and Stepanova gave up 'free art' in order to make things that, in their eyes, were more useful and more widely communicative: posters, books, architecture, clothing, furniture. In France, Ukraine-born Cassandre refrained from a career in painting because he rejected art as 'a game for the elite'. He, too, wanted to communicate with the masses. The artists who taught at the Bauhaus did not give up art altogether (and some returned to it after a prolific career in design) but they, too, were trying to find ways out of the arbitrariness and subjectivity inherent to free art.

If designers often choose to be designers because of a need to firmly prop up their image-making with objective specifications, demands and constraints, then those who choose to design type, instead of other objects or forms of communication, may have very deeply rooted reasons for doing so. If graphic design, in its functionalist, problem-solving guise, claims to be there to serve, then type design is there to serve those who serve. Paraphrasing singer Aimee Mann: Who, in his or her right creative mind, has so much ego to spare?

I have pondered over this aspect of type design for some time now and have come to the conclusion that many type designers have a legitimation issue. This could be an object of serious study. By unravelling self-constructed myths of originality, historical reference, ergonomics and legibility, economic and cultural relevance, and much more, one might get a grip on what makes type designers tick; on their motives for choosing a discipline of which only they, and a few expert users, fully appreciate the results.

I have come across some interesting cases. I already mentioned Adrian Frutiger, who has so often seemed desperate to justify work that, ultimately, requires no justification. I was fascinated – and often amused – by the passionate arguments of Evert Bloemsma. His untimely death in 2005 put an abrupt end to his discussions with a growing group of colleagues and friends, including myself, during the design processes of each of his typefaces. With Evert, self-justification was not something that happened after the fact. He was obsessed with functionality and innovation, and he was very moralistic about it. He felt that the only way to justify – justify what? The time spent on making fonts? No, justify releasing yet another typeface into the world, I guess – was by making sure that it was something genuinely new which that world had been waiting for; a solution to a real problem, even if very few people might have realized that a problem existed at all. His typeface FF Cocon has become a favourite for packaging, promising the softness and delight of commodities as diverse a low-calorie pudding, toothpaste and condoms; but preceding its release was a long period of worrying, speculating and having second thoughts about how to create a sans serif from which all hints of the written letter would have been eliminated. Evert would never have allowed himself to produce something as seemingly carefree and frivolous as Cocon without legitimizing it through the painstaking thinking process that preceded it.

Dutch design, male design

Erik Spiekermann has remarked that the Netherlands is the country with the highest density of type designers per square kilometre. Even though this may not be as obvious today as it was in the mid-1990s, the Netherlands is probably the country with the highest rate of unreleased typefaces. Well-made fonts that have remained unpublished, simply because their designers thought they were OK, but not good enough; or because they, like Evert Bloemsma, are still struggling to find legitimation for their work.

This may relate to what the Dutch call their Calvinist streak. It harks back to the bible-reading morality of Dutch Protestantism, which is somehow still palpable in the way in which the Dutch – especially those who 'make' things – often relate to their activities and products. They feel a kind of obligation to not just do a decent job, but to strive for perfection and to aim for optimum, no-frills utility; they inhabit, and help create, a universe in which beauty, as Eric Gill wrote, takes care of itself; where the beauty of a thing is a by-product of what it does.

The Dutch – and I think it is safe to generalize here – are extremely concerned with the way things work. They have little use for philosophy or abstraction. Many have one ongoing motivation in life: to find out how something works, analyse the process, and see how they can improve it. Men often prefer technical problems, while women focus on social processes. (This form of pragmatism does not always necessarily lead to efficiency: in groups, when everybody volunteers to be a fault-finder and a know-it-all, the results can be frustrating.)

Because of these and other 'national' characteristics, the Dutch have somewhat of a head start when choosing a career in type design. Pragmatism, perfectionism, a tough work ethic and a certain obsession with detail are qualities that are practically indispensable if one seriously intends to pursue a type designing career.

But the 'Dutchie' days are numbered. As more and more designers across the world are catching the type bug – with the new wave of interesting work from Latin America, for instance, a whole new region has come to the fore – our perceptions of what makes good type, and what makes a good designer, gradually change.

*

There's one thing that is changing only very, very slowly, and that is the male-to-female rate in type design. On a world-wide level, only a couple of women are in the top league, so to speak; and although among the runners-up the number of female type designers is clearly on the rise, the results don't compare to the strong position of women in graphic and communication design and adjacent fields. In some countries where type design traditionally has a strong presence, such as the UK and the Netherlands, the number of active female type designers is limited to less than a handful.

Is there a gender issue in type design? Houston-based Swiss designer Sibylle Hagmann, designer of the typefaces Cholla and Odile, thinks there is. In 2005, she published an article titled 'Non-existent design: women and the creation of type' (*Visual Communiation* 4). Trying to identify the factors causing 'gender imbalance' in type design she mentions, among other things, the lack of female role models and, both in education and in the typographic culture, a tendency to reflect male interests and sensibilities. She recommends measures such as 'adding more women's names to lists of conference speakers' and 'establishing a better network among female peers.'

The issue may partly be solving itself. In many design schools that focus on typography, the female students already outnumber the males. Female designers *are* getting exposure; as somewhat of an insider, I think it is safe to say that as soon as a female type designer has created a decent body of work (say, half a dozen typefaces) she is more likely to be interviewed in magazines and on blogs, or to be invited as a speaker, than her male counterpart who is in competition with male colleagues who have published twice as much. There is simply more curiosity about her. Thirdly, networks are taking shape. Hagmann herself is connected to Type Ladies, an informal platform initiated by Berlin designer Verena Gerlach with Veronika Burian, Elena Albertoni and Andrea Tinnes, among others.

*

There is a gender-related question linked to type design that Mrs Hagmann chooses not to touch on, but that I think is interesting. It is the question to what extent a discipline – any discipline – can be said to be typically male or typically female. Mind you – I'm not one to argue that all disciplines related to women's position in the traditional family are inherently feminine. But I do think there is a deeper layer of behaviour, a residue of the division of roles across the millennia that determines how we deal with tasks. Although I'm generally wary of bestsellers (30 million readers can't be right) John Gray's *Men Are from Mars, Women Are from Venus* contains some truisms that may pepper a discussion on gender 'equality' within the discipline of your choice. Mr. Gray points out that men are generally focused on individual problem-solving: it's what has always provided them with power over the situation, and dominance in the group while hunting or waging war. Women, who generally stayed at home to take care of complex tasks that required collaboration, such as agriculture and maintenance, focus on the social aspect of things. Few women are lone wolves; many men are, even when they think of themselves as team players.

Many relationships, private as well as professional, have been frustrated by these differences or a lack of understanding of them. However, that should not be a reason to get rid of the differences altogether. Quite possibly, women will always be more group-oriented and men will always be detail-obsessed geeks trying to make and repair stuff better and faster than the next guy. It is part of what makes us mutually interesting as partners. Is it a coincidence that type design fits so well with that anthropological/psychological picture of the nerdy repair man? What if type design is simply one of those activities that appeals to the male mindset more than to the female one?

I am not saying it should be a no-go area for women or a terrain where they cannot be at ease: some minds are more independent then others. And, as Hagmann writes, a stronger female presence will help expand our notion of what typography is, and help other woman find new role models. It is already happening: the recent popularity of script and handwriting fonts on MyFonts.com seems, for a large part, to have been instigated by women – on both the client and the designer side. But these are casual fonts for display or fun. The bulk of the workhorse types needed for newspapers or for meticulous book typography is still made – sorry, *developed* – by men. Some very exciting recent contributions to that field were made by women (like Hagmann's Odile or Burian's Maiola). But these are exceptions. The question is: Should we feel uncomfortable about that? I don't think so. Women are different, and so are men (that was the German title of the Mars/Venus book). If more men than women are attracted to type design, and especially to the design of geeky, technologically complex type systems, then so be it. Women may be able to make better use of those type systems to design something that communicates.

Aspect

CAPITALS

ABCDEƐFGGGHIJJKKLLMMNOPQQQQQRRRS
TUVWWWXYYZÀÁÂÃÄĀĂÅǺĄÆǼĆĈČĊÇĎ
ĐÈÉÊĚËĒĔĖĘÈÉÊĚËĒĔĖĘĜĞĠĢĜĞĠĢĜĞĠĢĤ
ĦÌÍÎĨÏĪĬĮIĲĴĴĶĶĹĽĻŁĿĹĽĻŁĿŃŇÑŅÒÓÔÕÖŌŎŐ
ØǾŒŔŘŖŔŘŖŔŘŖŚŜŠŞȘŤŢŦÙÚÛŨÜŪŬŮŰŲ
ẀẂŴẄẀẂŴẄẀẂŴẄỲÝŶŸỲÝŶŸŹŽŻŊĐ

LOWERCASE

aabbbbcdddddeeffgghhhhħħiıjkkkklll
lmmnnooppqqqqrrsttttuvwwxyyyzàáãäā
ăåǻąàáâãäāăåǻąæǽćĉčċçďđđèéêěëē
ĕėęèéêěëēĕėęĝğġģĝğġģĥħĥħħħìíîĩïīĭįıìíîĩ
ïīĭįıĳĵĵķķķķĺľŀļļłłłłńňñņńňñņòóôõö
ōŏőøǿœŕřŗŕřŗśŝšşșßťţŧţŧţŧţŧùúûũüūŭůű
ųẁẃŵẅẁẃŵẅỳýŷÿỳýŷÿỳýŷÿźžżŋðþþ

LIGATURES

LL NN OO TT Th Th ch ch ch ch ch ch ck ck ck ck
ck ck cl cl cl cl cl cl c ct ct ct ct ct ct e
fb fb fb fb ffb ffb ffb ffb ffb ffb ff ff ff fh fh fh fh fh
fh ffh ffh ffh ffh ffh ffh fi fi ffi ffi ffi fj fj ffj ffj ffj fk
fk fk fk ffk ffk ffk ffk ffk ffk fk fk ffk ffk fl fl
fl fl fl ffl ffl ffl fl fl ffl ffl ft ft ft ft fft fft fft ft
ft fft fft k k lb lb lk lk lk ll ll ll ll l l ll ll
lt lt lt oo oo pp rt sh sh sh sh sh sh sk sk sk sk
sk sk sl sl sl sl sl sl ss st st st st st st th
th tl t t tt tt

FIGURES, CURRENCY & RELATED FORMS

[DEFAULT] 0123456789€$¢£ƒ¥

[TABULAR] 0123456789€$£¥

[OLDSTYLE] 0123456789€$£¥

[TABULAR] 0123456789€$£¥

[SUPERIOR] 0123456789+−=() [INFERIOR] 0123456789+−=()

[NUMERATOR] 0123456789+−=() [DENOMINATOR] 0123456789+−=()

½ ⅓ ⅔ ¼ ¾ ⅕ ⅖ ⅗ ⅘ ⅙ ⅚ ⅛ ⅜ ⅝ ⅞

$\frac{1}{2}\frac{1}{3}\frac{2}{3}\frac{1}{4}\frac{1}{5}\frac{2}{5}\frac{3}{5}\frac{4}{5}\frac{1}{6}\frac{5}{6}\frac{1}{8}\frac{3}{8}\frac{5}{8}\frac{7}{8}$

+−±×÷=≠≈~^<>≤≥¬◊|¦∞∂∫√∆Ω∏∑µπ

⁄%‰№℮¤ℓ°ªº

PUNCTUATION & MARKS

'"'''""""‚„‹›‹›«»«».,:;…·!¡?¿

&&&&()()[][]{}{}\/*†‡§¶¶•#_-–—

@@@©℗®™

ACCENTS

` ´ ˆ ˇ ˜ ¨ ¯ ˘ ˚ ˝ ˙ ¸ ˛

Aspect™ has five weights
Light, Regular, Bold, ExtraBold, Heavy

ASPECT LIGHT 12 ON 16

LOREM IPSUM DOLOR sit amet, consectetuer adipiscing elit. Maecenas ut wisi at justo elementum gravida. Nulla tincidunt rhoncus erat. Donec non est ac velit semper gravida.

ASPECT REGULAR 12 ON 16

DONEC NON EST ac velit semper gravida. Suspendisse lobortis aliquam metus. Mauris purus lacus, auctor eu, dapibus sit amet, iaculis quis, elit. Sed a est. Donec et lectus at

ASPECT BOLD 12 ON 16

MORBI PURUS quam, consectetuer vitae, bibendum ut, feugiat eget, pede. Nullam posuere libero vel purus. Maecenas consectetuer cursus metus. Vestibulum lacus

ASPECT EXTRABOLD 12 ON 16

MAECENAS CONSECTETUER cursus metus. Vestibulum lacus augue, tempor eu, semper eu, tristique in, nunc. Donec accumsan nulla ac risus. Maecenas cursus lorem ut

ASPECT HEAVY 12 ON 16

DONEC ACCUMSAN nulla ac risus. Maecenas cursus lorem ut sapien. Nulla gravida eros sit amet nulla. Praesent mi. Aenean ut tortor. Donec accumsan nulla ac risus.

TELEPHONE

Talar þú ensku?

The long and the short

Dziękuję

Quieron un billete para Bilbao

water

MANY FINE WINES

Such formality was eventually abandoned

Bliss Pro Regular

LATIN CAPITALS

ABCDEFGHIJKLMNOPQRSTUVWXYZ

ÀÁÂÃÄĀĂÅǺĄÆǼĆĈČĊÇĎĐÈÉÊĚËĒ

ĔĖĘĜĞĠĢĤĦÌÍÎĨÏĪĬİĮĲĴĶĹĽĻŁĿŃŇÑŅ

ÒÓÔÕÖŌŎŐØǾŒŔŘŖŚŜŠŞȘŤŢŦÙÚÛ

ŨÜŪŬŮŰŲẀẂŴẄỲÝŶŸŹŽŻŊÐÞ

LATIN LOWERCASE

abcdefghijklmnopqrstuvwxyz

àáâãäāăåǻąæǽćĉčċçďđèéêěëēĕėęĝğġģ

ĥħìíîĩïīĭıįĳĵķĺľļłŀńňñņòóôõöōŏőøǿœŕřŗ

śŝšşșßťţŧùúûũüūŭůűųẁẃŵẅỳýŷÿźžżŋðþ

LATIN SMALL CAPITALS

ABCDEFGHIJKLMNOPQRSTUVWXYZ

ÀÁÂÃÄĀĂÅǺĄÆǼĆĈČĊÇĎĐÈÉÊĚËĒĔĖĘ

ĜĞĠĢĤĦÌÍÎĨÏĪĬİĮĲĴĶĹĽĻŁĿŃŇÑŅ

ÒÓÔÕÖŌŎŐØǾŒŔŘŖŚŜŠŞȘŤŢŦ

ÙÚÛŨÜŪŬŮŰŲẀẂŴẄỲÝŶŸŹŽŻŊÐÞ

SUPERIORS

abcdefghijklmnopqrstuvwxyz

Bliss Pro Italic

LATIN CAPITALS

ABCDEFGHIJKLMNOPQRSTUVWXYZ
ÀÁÂÃÄĀĂÅǺĄÆǼĆĈČĊÇĎĐÈÉÊĚËĒ
ĔĖĘĜĞĠĢĤĦÌÍÎĨÏĪĬĮIJĴĶĹĽĻŁĿŃŇÑŅ
ÒÓÔÕÖŌŎŐØǾŒŔŘŖŚŜŠŞȘŤŢŦÙÚÛ
ŨÜŪŬŮŰŲẀẂŴẄỲÝŶŸŹŽŻŊĐÞ

LATIN LOWERCASE

abcdefghijklmnopqrstuvwxyz
àáâãäāăåǻąæǽćĉčċçďđèéêěëēĕėęĝğġģ
ĥħìíîĩïīĭįıĳĵķĺľļłŀńňñņòóôõöōŏőøǿœŕřŗ
śŝšşșßťţŧùúûũüūŭůűųẁẃŵẅỳýŷÿźžżŋðþ

LATIN SMALL CAPITALS

ABCDEFGHIJKLMNOPQRSTUVWXYZ
ÀÁÂÃÄĀĂÅǺĄÆǼĆĈČĊÇĎĐÈÉÊĚËĒĔĖĘ
ĜĞĠĢĤĦÌÍÎĨÏĪĬĮIJĴĶĹĽĻŁĿŃŇÑŅ
ÒÓÔÕÖŌŎŐØǾŒŔŘŖŚŜŠŞȘŤŢŦ
ÙÚÛŨÜŪŬŮŰŲẀẂŴẄỲÝŶŸŹŽŻŊĐÞ

SUPERIORS

abcdefghijklmnopqrstuvwxyz

Bliss™ has seven weights plus italics
ExtraLight, Light, Regular, Medium, Bold, ExtraBold, Heavy

Bliss Pro Regular

GREEK CAPITALS

ΑΒΓΔΕΖΗΘΙΚΛΜΝΞΟΠΡΣΤΥΦΧΨΩ
ΆΈΉΊΪΌΎΫΏ

GREEK LOWERCASE

αβϐγδεζηθϑικλμνξοπρσςτυφϕχψω
άέήίϊΐόύϋΰώ

GREEK SMALL CAPITALS

ΑΒΓΔΕΖΗΘΙΚΛΜΝΞΟΠΡΣΤΥΦΧΨΩ
ΆΈΉΊΪΐΌΎΫΰΏ

CYRILLIC CAPITALS

АБВГЃҐДЂЕЀЁЄЖЅЗИЍЙІЇЈКЌЛЉМНЊ
ОПРСТЋУЎФѲХЦЏЧШЩЪЫЬѢЭЮЯѴ

CYRILLIC LOWERCASE

абδвгѓґдђеѐёєжѕзиѝйіїјкќлљмнњ
опрстћуўфѳхцџчшщъыьѣэюяѵ

CYRILLIC SMALL CAPITALS

АБВГЃҐДЂЕЀЁЄЖЅЗИЍЙІЇЈКЌЛЉМНЊ
ОПРСТЋУЎФѲХЦЏЧШЩЪЫЬѢЭЮЯѴ

Bliss Pro Italic

GREEK CAPITALS

ΑΒΓΔΕΖΗΘΙΚΛΜΝΞΟΠΡΣΤΥΦΧΨΩ

ΆΈΉΊΪΌΎΫΏ

GREEK LOWERCASE

αϐβγδεζηϑθικλμνξοπρσςτυφϕχψω

άέήίϊΐόύϋΰώ

GREEK SMALL CAPITALS

ΑΒΓΔΕΖΗΘΙΚΛΜΝΞΟΠΡΣΤΥΦΧΨΩ

ΆΈΉΊΪΪ́ΌΎΫΫ́Ώ

CYRILLIC CAPITALS

АБВГЃҐДЂЕЀЁЄЖЅЗИЍЙІЇЈКЌЛЉМНЊ

ОПРСТЋУЎФѲХЦЏЧШЩЪЫЬѢЭЮЯѴ

CYRILLIC LOWERCASE

абдвгѓґдђеѐёєжѕзиѝйіїјкќлљмнњ

опрстћуўфѳхцџчшщъыьѣэюяѵ

CYRILLIC SMALL CAPITALS

АБВГЃҐДЂЕЀЁЄЖЅЗИЍЙІЇЈКЌЛЉМНЊ

ОПРСТЋУЎФѲХЦЏЧШЩЪЫЬѢЭЮЯѴ

Bliss Pro Regular

FIGURES, CURRENCY & RELATED FORMS

[DEFAULT] 0123456789€$¢£ƒ¥

[TABULAR] 0123456789€$£¥

[OLDSTYLE] 0123456789€$£¥

[TABULAR] 0123456789€$£¥

[SMALL CAPITAL] 0123456789€$£¥

[SUPERIOR] 0123456789+−=() [INFERIOR] 0123456789+−=()

[NUMERATOR] 0123456789+−=() [DENOMINATOR] 0123456789+−=()

½ ⅓ ⅔ ¼ ¾ ⅕ ⅖ ⅗ ⅘ ⅙ ⅚ ⅛ ⅜ ⅝ ⅞

$\frac{1}{2}\frac{1}{3}\frac{2}{3}\frac{1}{4}\frac{3}{4}\frac{1}{5}\frac{2}{5}\frac{3}{5}\frac{4}{5}\frac{1}{6}\frac{5}{6}\frac{1}{8}\frac{3}{8}\frac{5}{8}\frac{7}{8}$

+−±×÷=≠≈~^<>≤≥¬◊|¦∞∂∫√ΔΩ∏∑µπ

/ % ‰ № ℮ ¤ ℓ ° ª º

PUNCTUATION & MARKS

'"‘’‘’“”“”‚„‹›‹›«»«».,:;…·!¡!¡?¿¿?¿

&&()()()[][][]{}{}{}\/*†‡§¶•#_-‐–−—―

@@@©©℗℗®™ [GREEK] ·;΄΅;

ACCENTS

` ` ´ ´ ^ ^ ˇ ˇ ˋ ~ ~ ¨ ¨ ¨ ¯ ¯ ˘ ˘ ˚ ˚ ˝ ˝ ˙ ˙ ¸ ˛ ¸ ˏ ΅ ˘ ˘

Bliss Pro Italic

FIGURES, CURRENCY & RELATED FORMS

[DEFAULT] *0123456789€$¢£ƒ¥*

[TABULAR] *0123456789€$£¥*

[OLDSTYLE] *0123456789€$£¥*

[TABULAR] *0123456789€$£¥*

[SMALL CAPITAL] *0123456789€$£¥*

[SUPERIOR] *0123456789+−=()* [INFERIOR] *0123456789+−=()*

[NUMERATOR] *0123456789+−=()* [DENOMINATOR] *0123456789+−=()*

½ ⅓ ⅔ ¼ ¾ ⅕ ⅖ ⅗ ⅘ ⅙ ⅚ ⅛ ⅜ ⅝ ⅞

1/2 1/3 2/3 1/4 3/4 1/5 2/5 3/5 4/5 1/6 5/6 1/8 3/8 5/8 7/8

+−±×÷=≠≈~^<>≤≥¬◊|¦∞∂∫√∆Ω∏∑µπ

/ % ‰ № ℮ ¤ ℓ ° ª º

PUNCTUATION & MARKS

' " ‘ ’ ‚ “ ” „ ‹ › ‹ › « » « » . , : ; … · ! ¡ ! ¡ ? ¿ ¿ ? ¿

*& & & & ( ) ( ) ( ) [ ] [ ] [ ] { } { } { } \ / * † ‡ § ¶ • # _ - - – – — —*

@ @ @ © © ℗ ℗ ® ™ [GREEK] *· ; ΄ ;*

ACCENTS

` ` ´ ´ ^ ^ ˇ ˇ ˜ ˜ ¨ ¨ ¯ ¯ ˘ ˘ ˚ ˚ ˝ ˝ ˙ ˙ ¸ ˛ ¸ ΄ ΅ ˘ ˘

Bliss Pro Latin

EXTRALIGHT 9 ON 12.5

QUISQUE DOLOR QUAM, pretium at, lacinia vel, varius at, odio. Curabitur mollis risus eget libero. Nullam nec dui in odio faucibus accumsan. Donec dictum vulputate ante. Pellentesque fringilla risus *mollis lacus. Nullam vestibulum nibh non wisi. Donec lobortis faucibus mauris. Vestibulum eu nisl in felis fermentum lobortis. Donec cursus*

LIGHT 9 ON 12.5

NUNC IN METUS. LOREM ipsum dolor sit amet, consectetuer adipiscing elit. Sed consequat. Fusce mollis libero ut lectus. Morbi et dolor. Proin nulla. Mauris felis. Praesent elementum tempus *nulla. Etiam interdum magna at ante. Praesent egestas dictum quam. Etiam leo metus, laoreet in, dictum et, nonummy eu, purus. Morbi*

REGULAR 9 ON 12.5

PULVINAR, DOLOR IN TEMPOR ALIQUAM, augue wisi placerat velit, vitae egestas purus lacus vel quam. Integer wisi. Praesent nec ante. Quisque porttitor imperdiet augue. Fusce placerat pharetra *velit. Ut lectus orci, cursus sed, tempus vel, condimentum a, lacus. Mauris quis lorem auctor nulla congue ultrices. Vivamus aliquam*

MEDIUM 9 ON 12.5

NISL AC NEQUE. VESTIBULUM NEC tortor et tortor eleifend dignissim. Quisque fringilla varius purus. Suspendisse mattis, arcu et iaculis dictum, eros mi interdum sem, nec lacinia turpis *ipsum nec est. Fusce mi. Suspendisse euismod vehicula quam. Cras tellus wisi, interdum vitae, aliquet eu, ultricies at, enim.*

BOLD 9 ON 12.5

QUISQUE NONUMMY CURSUS QUAM. Quisque congue. Morbi velit.Quisque augue sem, volutpat quis, feugiat a, semper ut, dolor. Nunc leo. Donec faucibus arcu vel risus blandit egestas. ***Vestibulum vestibulum. Aliquam luctus elementum felis. Etiam placerat. Nulla nisl. Nunc accumsan orci vitae erat. Aenean***

EXTRABOLD 9 ON 12.5

ACCUMSAN. PROIN VEL SEM NEC tortor bibendum sodales. Vestibulum vehicula. Aliquam pulvinar, sapien ut gravida iaculis, erat lorem interdum diam, quis placerat dui ante vel ***ipsum. Donec lobortis felis vel ligula. Pellentesque mauris. Nulla in odio. In bibendum pede et wisi. Nunc quis lorem non***

HEAVY 9 ON 12.5

TURPIS PHARETRA SAGITTIS. Suspendisse felis. Donec eleifend, mi quis sollicitudin auctor, diam magna commodo velit, at rutrum dolor ante id erat. Vivamus sollicitudin. Ut ***ac diam. Nam vel erat. Proin in pede. Sed vel turpis. Vestibulum vitae lacus. Cras a velit. Nunc dapibus hendrerit***

Proszę wezwać policję!

THE GREEN ROOM

March

upplýsingaþjónustu fyrir ferðafólk

Allegro

cantante lirica

Bliss Pro Greek

EXTRALIGHT 9 ON 12.5

ΕΠΕΙΔΗ Η ΑΝΑΓΝΩΡΙΣΗ ΤΗΣ αξιοπρέπειας, που είναι σύμφυτη σε όλα τα μέλη της ανθρώπινης οικογένειας, καθώς και των ίσων και αναπαλλοτρίωτων δικαιωμάτων τους αποτελεί το θεμέλιο της *ελευθερίας, της δικαιοσύνης και της ειρήνης στον κόσμο. Επειδή η παραγνώριση και η περιφρόνηση των δικαιωμάτων του ανθρώ-*

LIGHT 9 ON 12.5

ΠΟΥ ΟΔΗΓΗΣΑΝ ΣΕ ΠΡΑΞΕΙΣ ΒΑΡΒΑΡΟΤΗΤΑΣ, που εξεγείρουν την ανθρώπινη συνείδηση, και η προοπτική ενός κόσμου όπου οι άνθρωποι θα είναι ελεύθεροι να μιλούν και να πιστεύουν, *λυτρωμένοι από τον τρόμο και την αθλιότητα, έχει διακηρυχθεί ως η πιο υψηλή επιδίωξη του ανθρώπου. Επειδή έχει ουσιαστική*

REGULAR 9 ON 12.5

ΣΗΜΑΣΙΑ ΝΑ ΠΡΟΣΤΑΤΕΥΟΝΤΑΙ ΤΑ ανθρώπινα δικαιώματα από ένα καθεστώς δικαίου, ώστε ο άνθρωπος να μην αναγκάζεται να προσφεύγει, ως έσχατο καταφύγιο, στην εξέγερση κατά *της τυραννίας και της καταπίεσης. Επειδή έχει ουσιαστική σημασία να ενθαρρύνεται η ανάπτυξη φιλικών σχέσεων ανάμεσα*

MEDIUM 9 ON 12.5

ΣΤΑ ΕΘΝΗ. ΕΠΕΙΔΗ, ΜΕ ΤΟΝ καταστατικό Χάρτη, οι λαοί των Ηνωμένων Εθνών διακήρυξαν και πάλι την πίστη τους στα θεμελιακά δικαιώματα του ανθρώπου, στην αξιοπρέπεια *και την αξία της ανθρώπινης προσωπικότητας, στην ισότητα δικαιωμάτων ανδρών και γυναικών, και διακήρυξαν πως είναι*

BOLD 9 ON 12.5

ΑΠΟΦΑΣΙΣΜΕΝΟΙ ΝΑ ΣΥΝΤΕΛΕΣΟΥΝ στην κοινωνική πρόοδο και να δημιουργήσουν καλύτερες συνθήκες ζωής στα πλαίσια μιας ευρύτερης ελευθερίας. Επειδή τα κράτη μέλη ***ανέλαβαν την υποχρέωση να εξασφαλίσουν, σε συνεργασία με τον Οργανισμό των Ηνωμένων Εθνών, τον αποτελε-***

EXTRABOLD 9 ON 12.5

ΣΜΑΤΙΚΟ ΣΕΒΑΣΜΟ ΤΩΝ δικαιωμάτων του ανθρώπου και των θεμελιακών ελευθεριών σε όλο τον κόσμο. Επειδή η ταυτότητα αντιλήψεων ως προς τα δικαιώματα και τις ***ελευθερίες αυτές έχει εξαιρετική σημασία για να εκπληρωθεί πέρα ως πέρα αυτή η υποχρέωση. Διακηρύσσει ότι η***

HEAVY 9 ON 12.5

ΠΑΡΟΥΣΑ ΟΙΚΟΥΜΕΝΙΚΗ ΔΙΑΚΗΡΥΞΗ των Δικαιωμάτων του Ανθρώπου αποτελεί το κοινό ιδανικό στο οποίο πρέπει να κατατείνουν όλοι οι λαοί και όλα τα έθνη, έτσι ***ώστε κάθε άτομο και κάθε όργανο της κοινωνίας, με τη Διακήρυξη αυτή διαρκώς στη σκέψη, να καταβάλλει, με***

Λεξικό

Χάρτης της Ελλάδας

Βιβλίο

ΠΛΗΡΟΦΟΡΙΕΣ

Τα τελευταία Ελληνικά τραγούδια

Ταχυδρομείο

Bliss Pro Cyrillic

EXTRALIGHT 9 ON 12.5

Принимая во внимание, что признание достоинства, присущего всем членам человеческой семьи, и равных и неотъемлемых прав их является основой свободы, справедливости и *всеобщего мира; и принимая во внимание, что пренебрежение и презрение к правам человека привели к варварским актам,*

LIGHT 9 ON 12.5

которые возмущают совесть человечества, и что создание такого мира, в котором люди будут иметь свободу слова и убеждений и будут свободны от страха и нужды, провозглашено *как высокое стремление людей; и принимая во внимание, что необходимо, чтобы права человека охранялись властью*

REGULAR 9 ON 12.5

закона в целях обеспечения того, чтобы человек не был вынужден прибегать, в качестве последнего средства, к восстанию против тирании и угнетения; и принимая во внимание, *что необходимо содействовать развитию дружественных отношений между народами; и принимая во внимание, что*

MEDIUM 9 ON 12.5

народы Объединенных Наций подтвердили в Уставе свою веру в основные права человека, в достоинство и ценность человеческой личности и в равноправие мужчин и женщин *и решили содействовать социальному прогрессу и улучшению условий жизни при большей свободе; и принимая во*

BOLD 9 ON 12.5

внимание, что государствачлены обязались содействовать, в сотрудничестве с Организацией Объединенных Наций, всеобщему уважению и соблюдению прав человека *и основных свобод; и принимая во внимание, что всеобщее понимание характера этих прав и свобод имеет огромное*

EXTRABOLD 9 ON 12.5

значение для полного выполнения этого обязательства, провозглашает настоящую Всеобщую декларацию прав человека в качестве задачи, к выполнению которой должны *стремиться все народы и государства с тем, чтобы каждый человек и каждый орган общества, постоянно*

HEAVY 9 ON 12.5

имея в виду настоящую Декларацию, стремились путем просвещения и образования содействовать уважению этих прав и свобод и обеспечению, путем национальных *и международных прогрессивных мероприятий, всеобщего и эффективного признания и осуществления*

спасибо

СТОЯНКА ЗАПРЕЩЕНА!

Пожалуйста

Я благодарен Вам за помощь

Цветы

Большое спасибо за информацию

Я понимаю

Enigma Regular

CAPITALS

ABCDEFGHIJKLMNOPQRSTUVWXYZ
ÀÁÂÃÄĀĂÅǺĄÆǼĆĈČĊÇĎĐÈÉÊĚË
ĒĔĖĘĜĞĠĢĤĦÌÍÎĨÏĪĬİĮĲĴĶĹĽĻŁĿŃŇÑ
ŅÒÓÔÕÖŌŎŐØǾŒŔŘŖŚŜŠŞȘŤŢŦÙ
ÚÛŨÜŪŬŮŰŲẀẂŴẄỲÝŶŸŹŽŻŊÐÞ

LOWERCASE

abcdefghijklmnopqrstuvwxyz
àáâãäāăåǻąæǽćĉčċçďđèéêěëēĕ
ėęĝğġģĥħìíîĩïīĭįıĳĵķĺľļłŀńňñņò
óôõöōŏőøǿœŕřŗśŝšşșßťţŧùúû
ũüūŭůűųẁẃŵẅỳýŷÿźžżŋðþ

SMALL CAPITALS

ABCDEFGHIJKLMNOPQRSTUVWXYZ
ÀÁÂÃÄĀĂÅǺĄÆǼĆĈČĊÇĎĐÈÉÊĚËĒ
ĔĖĘĜĞĠĢĤĦÌÍÎĨÏĪĬĮĲĴĶĹĽĻŁĿŃŇÑŅ
ÒÓÔÕÖŌŎŐØǾŒŔŘŖŚŜŠŞȘŤŢŦÙÚÛ
ŨÜŪŬŮŰŲẀẂŴẄỲÝŶŸŹŽŻŊÐÞ

LIGATURES

fb ffb ff fh ffh fi ffi fj ffj fk ffk fl ffl

Enigma Italic

CAPITALS

ABCDEFGHIJKLMNOPQRSTUVWXYZ

ÀÁÂÃÄĀĂÅǺĄÆǼĆĈČĊÇĎĐÈÉÊĚË

ĒĔĖĘĜĞĠĢĤĦÌÍÎĨÏĪĬİĮĲĴĶĹĽĻŁĿŃŇÑ

ŅÒÓÔÕÖŌŎŐØǾŒŔŘŖŚŜŠŞȘŤŢŦÙÚ

ÛŨÜŪŬŮŰŲẀẂŴẄỲÝŶŸŹŽŻŊĐÞ

LOWERCASE

abcdefghijklmnopqrstuvwxyz

àáâãäāăåǻąæǽćĉčċçďđèéêěëēĕ

ėęĝğġģĥħìíîĩïīĭįıĳĵķĺľļłŀńňñņò

óôõöōŏőøǿœŕřŗśŝšşșßťţŧùúû

ũüūŭůűųẁẃŵẅỳýŷÿźžżŋðþ

SMALL CAPITALS

ABCDEFGHIJKLMNOPQRSTUVWXYZ

ÀÁÂÃÄĀĂÅǺĄÆǼĆĈČĊÇĎĐÈÉÊĚËĒ

ĔĖĘĜĞĠĢĤĦÌÍÎĨÏĪĬĮĲĴĶĹĽĻŁĿŃŇÑŅ

ÒÓÔÕÖŌŎŐØǾŒŔŘŖŚŜŠŞȘŤŢŦÙÚÛ

ŨÜŪŬŮŰŲẀẂŴẄỲÝŶŸŹŽŻŊĐÞ

LIGATURES

fb ffb ff fh ffh fi ffi fj ffj fk ffk fl ffl

Enigma™ has two weights plus italics
Regular, Bold

Enigma Regular

SUPERIORS

abcdefghijklmnopqrstuvwxyz

FIGURES, CURRENCY & RELATED FORMS

[DEFAULT] 0123456789€$¢£ƒ¥

[TABULAR] 0123456789€$£¥

[LINING] 0123456789€$£¥

[TABULAR] 0123456789€$£¥

[SUPERIOR] 0123456789+−=() [INFERIOR] 0123456789+−=()

[NUMERATOR] 0123456789+−=() [DENOMINATOR] 0123456789+−=()

+−±×÷=≠≈~^<>≤≥¬◊|¦∞∂∫√ΔΩ∏∑μπ

/ ¼½¾%‰№℮¤ℓ°ªº

PUNCTUATION & MARKS

'"‘’‚“”“”„„‹›‹›«»«».,:;…··!¡¡!¡?¿¿?¿

&&()()()[][][]{}{}{}\/*†‡§¶•#_-‐–—―

@@@©©℗℗®™

ACCENTS

` ` ´ ´ ˆ ˆ ˇ ˇ ¸ ˜ ˜ ¨ ¨ ¯ ¯ ˘ ˘ ˚ ˚ ˝ ˝ ˙ ˙

˛ ˛ ˛

Enigma Italic

SUPERIORS

abcdefghijklmnopqrstuvwxyz

FIGURES, CURRENCY & RELATED FORMS

[DEFAULT] 0123456789€$¢£ƒ¥

[TABULAR] 0123456789€$£¥

[LINING] 0123456789€$£¥

[TABULAR] 0123456789€$£¥

[SUPERIOR] 0123456789+-=() [INFERIOR] 0123456789+-=()

[NUMERATOR] 0123456789+-=() [DENOMINATOR] 0123456789+-=()

+−±×÷=≠≈~^<>≤≥¬◊|¦∞∂∫√ΔΩ∏∑µπ

/ ¼ ½ ¾ % ‰ № ℮ ¤ ℓ ° a o

PUNCTUATION & MARKS

'"‘’‚“”„«»‹›.,:;…·!¡?¿

&&()()()[][][]{}{}{}\/*†‡§¶•#_-‐–—―

@@@©©℗℗®™

ACCENTS

` ´ ^ ˇ ¸ ~ ¨ ¯ ˘ ˚ ˝ ˙

ENIGMA REGULAR 9 ON 11

MORBI QUAM. PRAESENT INTERDUM ORCI. Morbi non velit feugiat pede rhoncus commodo. Cras est sem, consectetuer eu, volutpat in, ultrices vel, lectus. Sed vitae diam in mauris dictum eleifend. Class aptent taciti sociosqu ad litora torquent per conubia nostra, per inceptos hymenaeos. Sed at magna malesuada lacus posuere accumsan. Suspendisse porttitor posuere lectus. Nulla egestas placerat velit. Etiam pellentesque. Nunc dui dui, auctor quis, elementum in, bibendum eu, justo. Mauris auctor ultric-

ENIGMA ITALIC 9 ON 11

SUSPENDISSE TEMPOR. IN CURSUS GRAVIDA ODIO. Mauris ac dolor. Curabitur mattis. Praesent massa purus, eleifend in, tempor id, porta at, lacus. Nam quis quam. Maecenas sagittis odio eget est. Morbi justo ipsum, mollis et, sollicitudin pellentesque, interdum facilisis, nibh. Nunc convallis ipsum a sem. Nullam ante odio, interdum eu, scelerisque in, aliquet vel, mi. Vestibulum non nunc. Nullam sed lacus sed urna pulvinar lobortis. Nullam vehicula turpis at dolor. Cras vitae mauris sed mi gravida auctor. Morbi tortor diam, convallis eu, tristique et, congue a,

ENIGMA BOLD 9 ON 11

AENEAN SAPIEN ODIO, DICTUM ID, BLANDIT non, nonummy eget, velit. Quisque id pede. Sed posuere tempor turpis. Curabitur fermentum, arcu vitae laoreet dignissim, lectus est consequat wisi, at molestie lorem leo sed pede. Pellentesque at lacus id mauris iaculis consequat. Mauris eu nulla vel eros faucibus accumsan. Sed sodales interdum metus. Nullam semper eros a libero. Aenean nonummy dolor ac pede. Nulla vitae dolor eu dui rhoncus congue. Suspendisse potenti. Donec vitae nunc

ENIGMA BOLD ITALIC 9 ON 11

IN HAC HABITASSE PLATEA DICTUMST. In hac habitasse platea dictumst. Aenean libero diam, tristique at, imperdiet ac, interdum quis, libero. Etiam vel ipsum. Nulla sapien leo, elementum nec, interdum at, faucibus at, ante. Sed scelerisque. Vestibulum rutrum tellus nec lorem. Vivamus tincidunt, ligula id dictum adipiscing, sem elit adipiscing diam, eget vestibulum justo risus id justo. Pellentesque habitant morbi tristique senectus et netus et malesuada fames ac turpis egestas. Curabitur lacinia sodales enim. Nullam sollicitudin lectus porta eros. In lobortis diam sed

* 7 *

PENGUINS ABROAD

THE paper-back is regarded as the most spectacular phenomenon in American publishing. All the chroniclers of its development there agree that the story begins with the first tentative export from this country of some of the early Penguins. An American branch of Penguin Books Ltd was established in 1939; and, because of the war cut off supplies from this country, the American branch began to select and publish its own titles. It soon became clear that the conception of the American Penguin differed fundamentally from the British one and, several compromises having proved ineffectual, the American partnership was dissolved, and the Penguin symbol reverted to wholly British ownership. In 1950 Penguin Books Ltd launched its own company in America, and Penguin Books Inc. opened its base in Baltimore.

One of the differences which had developed between Penguins and its American associates concerned the market which Penguins should seek in the U.S.A. The Americans wanted the mass market in terms of quarter million sales or more, for every title. This market could not be reached through bookshops alone, for

Example in Enigma Regular (after Hans Schmoller)

ENIGMA REGULAR 14 ON 17

MAECENAS AT NISL QUIS JUSTO ornare luctus. Aenean et risus vel metus consequat suscipit. Aliquam erat volutpat. Donec pellentesque wisi quis ligula. Nunc vitae quam sit amet augue porta tincidunt.

ENIGMA ITALIC 14 ON 17

SUSPENDISSE ET LIBERO. ETIAM VITAE dolor. Praesent dapibus blandit arcu. Nulla lacus. Nullam faucibus laoreet nisl. Fusce ut quam. Vivamus in nibh. In vehicula turpis eget ligula. Cras cursus imperdiet erat. Phasellus nec lorem.

ENIGMA BOLD 14 ON 17

NULLA BLANDIT SUSCIPIT LIGULA. Vestibulum id sapien semper lectus vestibulum imperdiet. Nam varius faucibus metus. Mauris consequat tristique quam. Suspendisse in pede. Praesent dignissim

ENIGMA BOLD ITALIC 14 ON 17

QUISQUE DOLOR QUAM, PRETIUM at, lacinia vel, varius at, odio. Curabitur mollis risus eget libero. Nullam nec dui in odio faucibus accumsan. Donec dictum vulputate ante. Pellentesque fringilla risus mollis lacus. Nullam

CONTENTS

Example in Enigma Regular and Italic (after W A Dwiggins)

Kingfisher Regular

CAPITALS

ABCDEFGHIJKLMNOPQRSTUVWXYZ
ÀÁÂÃÄĀĂÅǺĄÆǼĆĈČĊÇĎĐÈÉÊĚËĒ
ĔĖĘĜĞĠĢĤĦÌÍÎĨÏĪĬİĮĲĴĶĹĽĻŁĿŃŇÑŅ
ÒÓÔÕÖŌŎŐØǾŒŔŘŖŚŜŠŞȘŤŢŦÙÚ
ÛŨÜŪŬŮŰŲẀẂŴẄỲÝŶŸŹŽŻŊĐÞ

LOWERCASE

abcdefghijklmnopqrstuvwxyz
àáâãäāăåǻąæǽćĉčċçďđèéêěëēĕėęĝğġģ
ĥħìíîĩïīĭįıĳĵķĺľļłŀńňñņòóôõöōŏőøǿœŕřŗ
śŝšşșßťţŧùúûũüūŭůűųẁẃŵẅỳýŷÿźžżŋðþ

SMALL CAPITALS

ABCDEFGHIJKLMNOPQRSTUVWXYZ
ÀÁÂÃÄĀĂÅǺĄÆǼĆĈČĊÇĎĐÈÉÊĚËĒĔĖĘ
ĜĞĠĢĤĦÌÍÎĨÏĪĬİĮĲĴĶĹĽĻŁĿŃŇÑŅ
ÒÓÔÕÖŌŎŐØǾŒŔŘŖŚŜŠŞȘŤŢŦ
ÙÚÛŨÜŪŬŮŰŲẀẂŴẄỲÝŶŸŹŽŻŊĐÞ

LIGATURES & SWASH ELEMENTS

fb ffb ff fh ffh fi ffi fj ffj fk ffk fl ffl fþ

Kingfisher Italic

CAPITALS

ABCDEFGHIJKLMNOPQRSTUVWXYZ
ÀÁÂÃÄĀĂÅǺĄÆǼĆĈČĊÇĎĐÈÉÊĚËĒ
ĔĖĘĜĞĠĢĤĦÌÍÎĨÏĪĬİĮĲĴĶĹĽĻŁĿŃŇÑŅ
ÒÓÔÕÖŌŎŐØǾŒŔŘŖŚŜŠŞȘŤŢŦÙÚ
ÛŨÜŪŬŮŰŲẀẂŴẄỲÝŶŸŹŽŻŊĐÞ

LOWERCASE

abcdefghijklmnopqrstuvwxyz
àáâãäāăåǻąæǽćĉčċçďđèéêěëēĕėęĝğġģ
ĥħìíîĩïīĭįıĳĵķĺľļłŀńňñņòóôõöōŏőøǿœŕřŗ
śŝšşșßťţŧùúûũüūŭůűųẁẃŵẅỳýŷÿźžżŋðþ

SMALL CAPITALS

ABCDEFGHIJKLMNOPQRSTUVWXYZ
ÀÁÂÃÄĀĂÅǺĄÆǼĆĈČĊÇĎĐÈÉÊĚËĒĔĖĘ
ĜĞĠĢĤĦÌÍÎĨÏĪĬİĮĲĴĶĹĽĻŁĿŃŇÑŅ
ÒÓÔÕÖŌŎŐØǾŒŔŘŖŚŜŠŞȘŤŢŦ
ÙÚÛŨÜŪŬŮŰŲẀẂŴẄỲÝŶŸŹŽŻŊĐÞ

LIGATURES & SWASH ELEMENTS

fb ffb ff fh ffh fi ffi fj ffj fk ffk fl ffl fþ
gf gfi gfl

Kingfisher™ has three weights and a Display variant plus italics
Regular, Bold, Heavy, Display

Kingfisher Regular

SUPERIORS

abcdefghijklmnopqrstuvwxyz

FIGURES, CURRENCY & RELATED FORMS

[DEFAULT] 0123456789€$¢£ƒ¥

[TABULAR] 0123456789€$£¥

[LINING] 0123456789€$£¥

[TABULAR] 0123456789€$£¥

[SMALL CAPITAL] 0123456789€$£¥

[SUPERIOR] 0123456789+-=() [INFERIOR] 0123456789+-=()

[NUMERATOR] 0123456789+-=() [DENOMINATOR] 0123456789+-=()

½ ⅓ ⅔ ¼ ¾ ⅕ ⅖ ⅗ ⅘ ⅙ ⅚ ⅛ ⅜ ⅝ ⅞

$\frac{1}{2}\frac{1}{3}\frac{2}{3}\frac{1}{4}\frac{3}{4}\frac{1}{5}\frac{2}{5}\frac{3}{5}\frac{4}{5}\frac{1}{6}\frac{5}{6}\frac{1}{8}\frac{3}{8}\frac{5}{8}\frac{7}{8}$

+−±×÷=≠≈~^<>≤≥¬◊|¦∞∂∫√∆Ω∏∑µπ

⁄ % ‰ № ℮ ¤ ℓ ° ª º

PUNCTUATION & MARKS

' " ‘ ’ ‚ “ ” “ ” „ ‹ › ‹ › « » « » . , : ; … · ! ¡ ¡ ! ¡ ? ¿ ¿ ? ¿

& & ( ) ( ) ( ) [ ] [ ] [ ] { } { } { } \ / * † ‡ § ¶ • # _ - - – – — —

@ @ @ © © ℗ ℗ ® ™

ACCENTS

` ` ´ ´ ˆ ˆ ˇ ˇ ' ˜ ˜ ¨ ¨ ¯ ¯ ˘ ˘ ˚ ˚ ˝ ˝ ˙ ˙

¸ ˛ ,

Kingfisher Italic

SUPERIORS

abcdefghijklmnopqrstuvwxyz

FIGURES, CURRENCY & RELATED FORMS

[DEFAULT] *0123456789€$¢£ƒ¥*

[TABULAR] *0123456789€$£¥*

[LINING] *0123456789€$£¥*

[TABULAR] *0123456789€$£¥*

[SMALL CAPITAL] *0123456789€$£¥*

[SUPERIOR] *0123456789+-=()* [INFERIOR] *0123456789+-=()*

[NUMERATOR] *0123456789+-=()* [DENOMINATOR] *0123456789+-=()*

½ ⅓ ⅔ ¼ ¾ ⅕ ⅖ ⅗ ⅘ ⅙ ⅚ ⅛ ⅜ ⅝ ⅞

1/2 1/3 2/3 1/4 3/4 1/5 2/5 3/5 4/5 1/6 5/6 1/8 3/8 5/8 7/8

+−±×÷=≠≈~^<>≤≥¬◊|¦∞∂∫√ΔΩΠ∑µπ

⁄ % ‰ № ℮ ¤ ℓ ° ª º

PUNCTUATION & MARKS

' " ‘ ’ ‚ “ ” “ ” „ ‹ › ‹ › « » « » . , : ; … · ! ¡ ! ¡ ? ¿ ¿ ? ¿

& & ( ) ( ) ( ) [ ] [ ] [ ] { } { } { } \ / * † ‡ § ¶ • # _ - ‐ – − — —

@ @ @ © © ℗ ℗ ® ™

ACCENTS

` ` ´ ´ ˆ ˆ ˇ ˇ ˜ ˜ ¨ ¨ ¯ ¯ ˘ ˘ ˚ ˚ ˝ ˝ ˙ ˙

¸ ˛ ,

One of the 'Holy Grails' within type design is the production of a typeface, which manages to capture the colour, vitality, interest and stature of predecessors from the history of printing. Such a search is not new. The Private Press movement in England saw the creation of many custom typefaces derived from much older models, most notably the famous early types of Nicolas Jenson.

The human eye registers an incredible amount of detail as it scans. The trick is to design a type that has just the right amount of interest for the eye without distracting it from its primary function – to collect the text and deliver it to the brain to be understood. If a type overwhelms with ideas of beauty, or too much quirky originality, or is just outstandingly different, then it functions less well as a text type and is better suited to display contexts. Conversely if a type has too little aesthetic detailing or formal interest, it can become monotonous to view causing the eye and mind to wander. Additional influences affect this too but these are generally beyond the scope of the type designer.

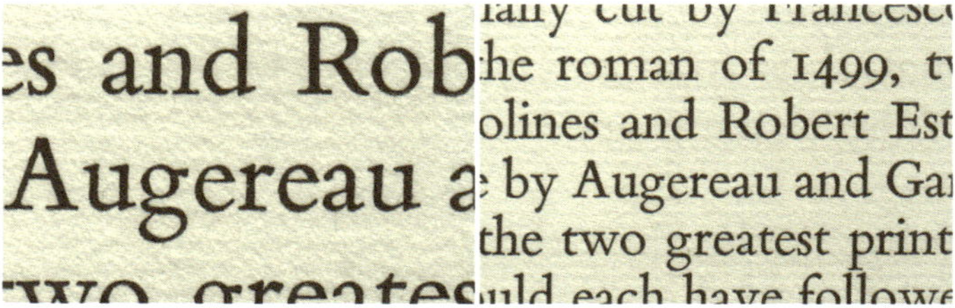

Original Monotype Bembo (series 270) 1929
Several historic typefaces were studied with special attention given to the printed effect. When handled and printed well, letterpress Bembo is outstanding. Not bad for a typeface based on a model from 1495

The concept of making text type interesting to the eye, and in so doing make the reading experience a better one, has been discussed many times. An interesting view is that the punchcutter was well aware of the need for subtle irregularities in the letterforms he cut. It could be suggested that these irregularities break the systematic monotony of the reading experience. The theory is that character irregularities will, when the type is set, give the text a lively pattern, nothing startling, but with just enough interest to entice the eye. Perhaps, today the irregularities of punchcutting, once lost to industrialization, could be reintroduced in an attempt to reinvigorate the reading experience. This idea was developed through the design of Kingfisher. A slight irregularity has been added to the letters to make the overall flow of the type seem less rigid. Several of the lowercase letters, for example, incorporate a varied degree of movement and the illusion of a slight slope has been added to the verticals. All this imparts a very subtle restlessness to the text.

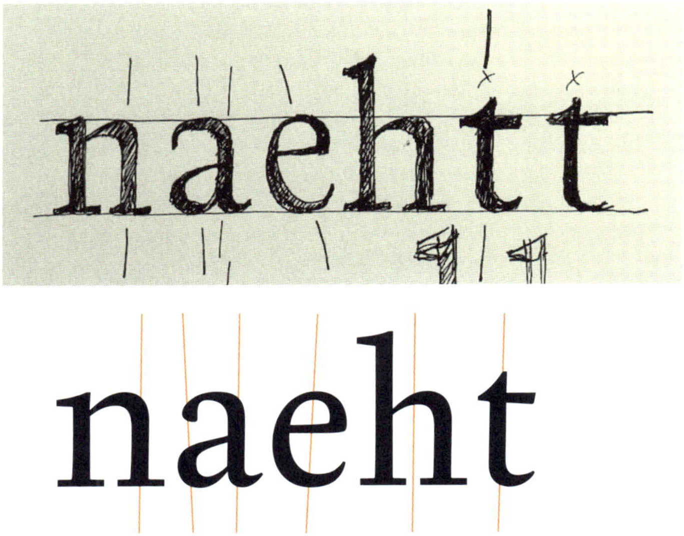

A slight irregularity to the letters help make the overall flow of the type seem less rigid

KINGFISHER REGULAR 8 ON 11

PROIN QUIS NULLA AT VELIT facilisis dignissim. Suspendisse nonummy purus quis lorem. Vivamus eu dolor id ullamcorper sollicitudin. Cras rutrum lacinia erat. Mauris neque sapien, venenatis ut, condimentum ut, venenatis vel, metus. Morbi ac ligula. Proin quis ante vel sapien volutpat ornare. Nulla *rhoncus condimentum nibh. Pellentesque sed mi. Morbi lobortis, urna mattis vestibulum mollis, elit dolor condimentum risus, a sollicitudin felis sapien in libero. Praesent hendrerit malesuada mi. Sed ornare euismod mauris. Nam laoreet ante eu risus. Nam porttitor justo. Aliquam sit amet neque nec metus mollis rhoncus.*

KINGFISHER BOLD 8 ON 11

NUNC UT MAURIS ID LOREM elementum fringilla. Nulla consequat, lacus dignissim lacinia auctor, dui nunc lacinia felis, non egestas massa erat vitae ante. Duis ornare bibendum turpis. Morbi nunc. Nulla facilisi. Pellentesque fringilla odio pulvinar sapien. Praesent pulvinar, leo quis viverra ***ullamcorper, libero arcu congue dui, et tempus wisi tortor ut mauris. Morbi in odio pharetra felis cursus feugiat. Nulla pede. Integer volutpat ornare mauris. Cras dapibus accumsan quam. Pellentesque dui sapien, condimentum id, gravida placerat, venenatis ut, dui. Quisque justo leo, iaculis sit amet, aliquet sed,***

KINGFISHER HEAVY 8 ON 11

INTEGER EGESTAS NULLA. Vestibulum id pede quis augue mattis condimentum. Etiam purus tortor, accumsan vitae, condimentum et, mollis eu, eros. Ut ligula leo, ullamcorper id, molestie sagittis, dignissim id, ante. Vivamus wisi. Sed tempus feugiat massa. Aenean vulputate scelerisque lorem. ***Sed rutrum malesuada felis. Aliquam erat volutpat. Nulla lacinia lorem ac turpis. Sed pulvinar. Aliquam eget turpis eget lacus laoreet facilisis. Sed tellus. Donec lobortis pulvinar dui. Phasellus hendrerit suscipit velit. Ut auctor, wisi vel sagittis lobortis, libero mauris dignissim massa, ut quam libero eu erat.***

JUSTIFICATION

Reprinted from the first edition of Edward FitzGerald's translation:

RUBÁIYÁT ‖ OF ‖ OMAR KHAYYÁM, ‖
THE ASTRONOMER-POET OF PERSIA. ‖
TRANSLATED INTO ENGLISH VERSE. ‖
[rule] ‖ LONDON: ‖ BERNARD QUARITCH, ‖
CASTLE STREET, LEICESTER SQUARE. ‖
1859.

Printed by
Joh. Enschedé en Zonen
Haarlem
for
A. A. Balkema
Amsterdam
1945

Example in Kingfisher Regular and Italic (after Jan van Krimpen)

KINGFISHER REGULAR 10 ON 13

PELLENTESQUE ELEMENTUM, ipsum nec porta iaculis, mi wisi dictum ipsum, vel pellentesque orci neque ut nibh. Maecenas tincidunt nulla sit amet dui. In hac habitasse platea dictumst. Duis ante. Pellentesque diam ipsum, dapibus laoreet, fringilla vel, consectetuer non, mauris. *Pellentesque urna. Donec velit lacus, fringilla ac, nonummy eget, eleifend ut, augue. Aenean venenatis enim eu enim. Curabitur eleifend posuere neque. Proin a mauris. Praesent dignissim mi id dui. Praesent ultrices justo ac turpis. Nullam*

KINGFISHER BOLD 10 ON 13

IN HAC HABITASSE PLATEA DICTUMST. Morbi dolor ligula, semper eu, adipiscing ut, consequat vitae, sapien. Nullam rhoncus. Nullam risus. Suspendisse leo aliquam erat volutpat. Maecenas fringilla feugiat tortor. Morbi nulla tortor, dignissim vel, varius et, aliquam et, eros. ***Etiam non nisl. Etiam nonummy, velit et sodales sodales, eros metus accumsan eros, at pharetra lorem a mauris. Mauris risus erat, convallis dictum, lacinia at, dignissim non, magna. Nulla facilisi. Suspendisse tortor elit,***

KINGFISHER HEAVY 10 ON 13

CURABITUR LIGULA NEQUE, viverra a, commodo sed, venenatis in, justo. Morbi consectetuer aliquet lacus. Cras ut tellus. Phasellus malesuada vulputate diam. Sed ut libero vel quam luctus varius. Quisque pulvinar felis sed ante commodo tincidunt. Sed congue turpis non ***libero. Proin cursus, pede eu rhoncus vulputate, tortor enim ultrices velit, ut sagittis lorem erat at lectus. Morbi sit amet elit in neque placerat convallis. Cras elit sapien, fringilla sed, imperdiet ut, malesuada vel, mi. Fusce***

MARIA: No.
BOYET: What then, do you see?
ROSALINE: Ay, our way to be gone.
BOYET: You are too hard for me.

Exeunt.

III.1

Enter Braggart and Boy.

Song.

BRAGGART: Warble child, make passionate my sense of hearing.

BOY: Concolinel.

BRAGGART: Sweet air, go tenderness of years: take this key, give enlargement to the swain, bring him festinately hither: I must employ him in a letter to my love.

BOY: Will you win your love with a French brawl?

BRAGGART: How meanst thou, brawling in French?

BOY: No my complete master, but to jig off a tune at the tongue's end, canary to it with the feet, humour it with turning up your eye: sigh a note and sing a note, sometime through the throat: as if you swallow'd love with singing love, sometime through the nose as if you snuff'd up love by smelling love with your hat penthouse-like o'er the shop of your eyes, with your arms cross'd on your thinbelly boublet, like a rabbit on a spit, or your hands in your pocket, like a man after the old painting, and keep not too long in one tune, but a snip and away: these are complements, these are humours, these betray nice wenches that would be betrayed without these, and make them men of note: do you note men that most are affected to these?

BRAGGART: How hast thou purchased this experience?

Example in Kingfisher Regular (after Jan Tschichold)

KINGFISHER DISPLAY

Science Fiction

Crime

Biographies

ARCHITECTURE

Art & Design

Music

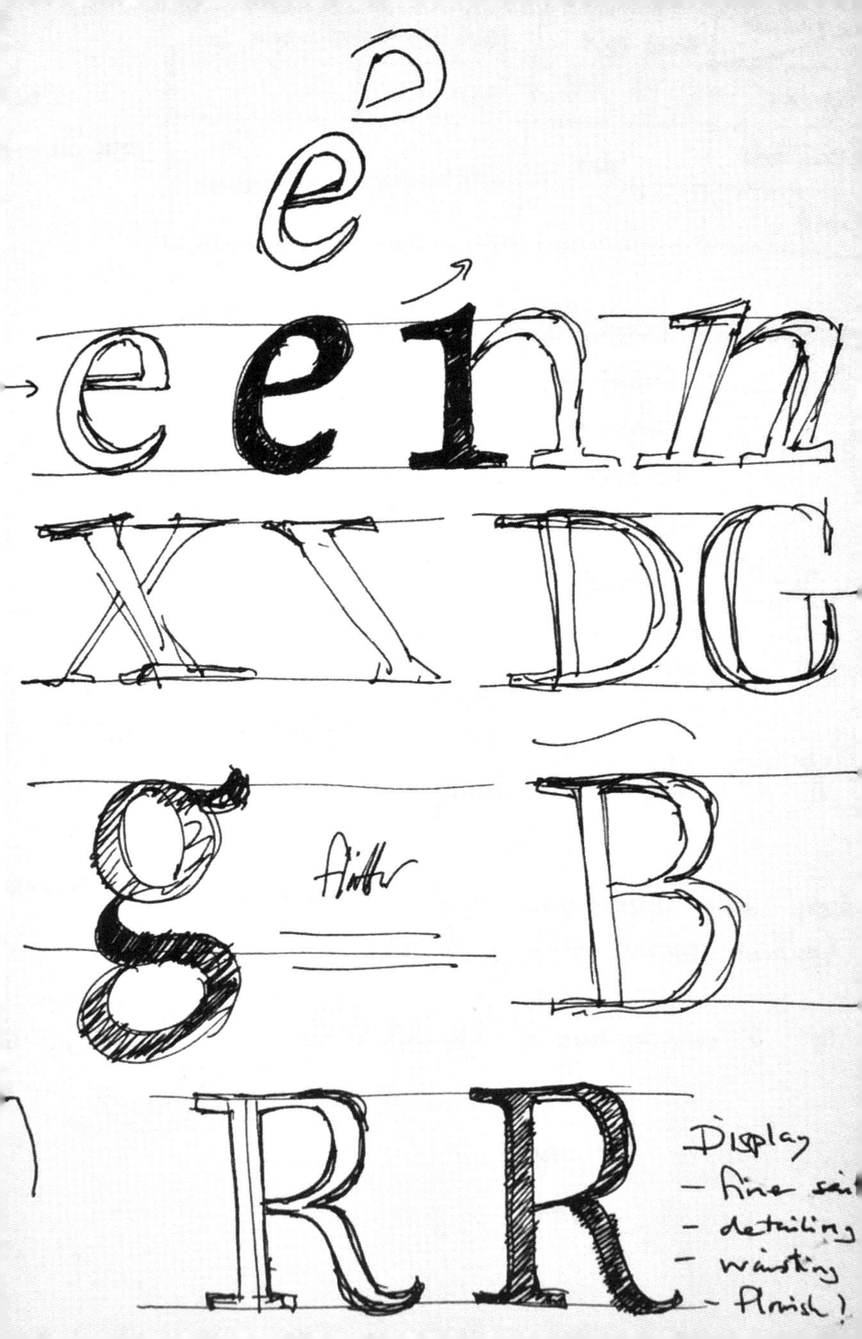

Display
- fine
- detailing
- waisting
- flourish!

Shaker Regular

CAPITALS

ABCDEFGHIJKLMNOPQRSTUVWXYZ
ÀÁÂÃÄĀĂÅǺĄÆǼĆĈČĊÇĎĐÈÉÊĚËĒ
ĔĖĘĜĞĠĢĤĦÌÍÎĨÏĪĬĮIJĴĶĹĽĻŁĿŃŇÑŅÒ
ÓÔÕÖŌŎŐØǾŒŔŘŖŚŜŠŞȘŤŢŦÙÚÛ
ŨÜŪŬŮŰŲẀẂŴẄỲÝŶŸŹŽŻŊĐÞ

LOWERCASE

abcdefghijklmnopqrstuvwxyzàáâãäā
ăåǻąæǽćĉčċçďđèéêěëēĕėęĝğġģĥħìíîĩï
īĭįıijĵķĺľļłŀńňñņòóôõöōŏőøǿœŕřŗśŝšşș
ßťţŧùúûũüūŭůűųẁẃŵẅỳýŷÿźžżŋðþ

SMALL CAPITALS

ABCDEFGHIJKLMNOPQRSTUVWXYZÀÁÂÃÄ
ĀĂÅǺĄÆǼĆĈČĊÇĎĐÈÉÊĚËĒĔĖĘĜĞĠĢĤĦÌÍÎĨÏ
ĪĬĮIJĴĶĹĽĻŁĿŃŇÑŅÒÓÔÕÖŌŎŐØǾŒŔŘŖŚŜŠŞ
ȘŤŢŦÙÚÛŨÜŪŬŮŰŲẀẂŴẄỲÝŶŸŹŽŻŊĐÞ

LIGATURES

fb ffb ff fh ffh fi ffi fj ffj fk ffk fl ffl

Shaker Italic

CAPITALS

ABCDEFGHIJKLMNOPQRSTUVWXYZ
ÀÁÂÃÄĀĂÅǺĄÆǼĆĈČĊÇĎĐÈÉÊĚËĒ
ĔĖĘĜĞĠĢĤĦÌÍÎĨÏĪĬİĮIJĴĶĹĽĻŁĿŃŇÑŅÒ
ÓÔÕÖŌŎŐØǾŒŔŘŖŚŜŠŞȘŤȚŦÙÚÛ
ŨÜŪŬŮŰŲẀẂŴẄỲÝŶŸŹŽŻŊĐÞ

LOWERCASE

abcdefghijklmnopqrstuvwxyzàáâãäā
ăåǻąæǽćĉčċçďđèéêěëēĕėęĝğġģĥħìíîĩï
īĭįıijĵķĺľļłŀńňñņòóôõöōŏőøǿœŕřŗśŝšşș
ßťțŧùúûũüūŭůűųẁẃŵẅỳýŷÿźžżŋðþ

SMALL CAPITALS

ABCDEFGHIJKLMNOPQRSTUVWXYZÀÁÂÃÄ
ĀĂÅǺĄÆǼĆĈČĊÇĎĐÈÉÊĚËĒĔĖĘĜĞĠĢĤĦÌÍÎĨÏ
ĪĬĮIJĴĶĹĽĻŁĿŃŇÑŅÒÓÔÕÖŌŎŐØǾŒŔŘŖŚŜŠŞ
ȘŤȚŦÙÚÛŨÜŪŬŮŰŲẀẂŴẄỲÝŶŸŹŽŻŊĐÞ

LIGATURES

fb ffb ff fh ffh fi ffi fj ffj fk ffk fl ffl

Shaker™ has five weights plus italics
Light, Regular, Bold, ExtraBold, Heavy
available in three widths Condensed, Regular, Wide

Shaker Regular

SUPERIORS

abcdefghijklmnopqrstuvwxyz

FIGURES, CURRENCY & RELATED FORMS

[DEFAULT] 0123456789€$¢£ƒ¥

[TABULAR] 0123456789€$£¥

[LINING] 0123456789€$£¥

[TABULAR] 0123456789€$£¥

[SUPERIOR] 0123456789+-=() [INFERIOR] 0123456789+-=()

[NUMERATOR] 0123456789+-=() [DENOMINATOR] 0123456789+-=()

+−±×÷=≠≈~^<>≤≥¬◊|¦∞∂∫√ΔΩ∏∑µπ

/ ¼ ½ ¾ % ‰ № ℮ ¤ ℓ ° a o

PUNCTUATION & MARKS

'"''‚,""""„„‹›‹›«»«».,:;…·!¡!¡?¿?¿

&&()()()[][][]{}{}{}\/*†‡§¶•#_-‐–—―

@@@©©℗℗®™

ACCENTS

` ` ´ ´ ^ ^ ˇ ˇ ˜ ˜ ¨ ¨ ¯ ¯ ˘ ˘ ˚ ˚ ˝ ˝ ˙ ˙ ¸ ˛ ,

Shaker Italic

SUPERIORS

abcdefghijklmnopqrstuvwxyz

FIGURES, CURRENCY & RELATED FORMS

[DEFAULT] *0123456789€$¢£ƒ¥*

[TABULAR] *0123456789€$£¥*

[LINING] *0123456789€$£¥*

[TABULAR] *0123456789€$£¥*

[SUPERIOR] *0123456789+-=()* [INFERIOR] *0123456789+-=()*

[NUMERATOR] *0123456789+-=()* [DENOMINATOR] *0123456789+-=()*

+−±×÷=≠≈~^<>≤≥¬◊|¦∞∂∫√ΔΩ∏∑µπ

/ ¼ ½ ¾ % ‰ № ℮ ¤ ℓ ° a o

PUNCTUATION & MARKS

' " ' ' ‚ ' " " " " „ ‹ › ‹ › « » « » . , : ; … · ! ¡ ! ¡ ? ¿ ? ¿

& & ( ) ( ) ( ) [ ] [ ] [ ] { } { } { } \ / * † ‡ § ¶ • # _ - - - – — —

@ @ @ © © ℗ ℗ ® ™

ACCENTS

` ` ´ ´ ^ ^ ˇ ˇ ˜ ˜ ¨ ¨ ¯ ¯ ˘ ˘ ˚ ˚ ˝ ˝ ˙ ˙ ¸ ˛ ,

Shaker Condensed

SHAKER LIGHT CONDENSED & ITALIC 11 ON 14

MORBI QUAM. PRAESENT INTERDUM ORCI. Morbi non velit feugiat pede rhoncus commodo. Cras est sem, consectetuer eu, volutpat in, ultrices vel, lectus. Sed vitae diam in mauris dictum eleifend. Class *aptent taciti sociosqu ad litora torquent per conubia nostra, per inceptos hymenaeos. Sed at magna malesuada lacus posuere accumsan. Sus-*

SHAKER CONDENSED & ITALIC 11 ON 14

SUSPENDISSE TEMPOR. In cursus gravida odio. Mauris ac dolor. Curabitur mattis. Praesent massa purus, eleifend in, tempor id, porta at, lacus. Nam quis quam. Maecenas sagittis odio eget est. Morbi justo *ipsum, mollis et, sollicitudin pellentesque, interdum facilisis, nibh. Nunc convallis ipsum a sem. Nullam ante odio, interdum eu, scelerisque in, ali-*

SHAKER BOLD CONDENSED & ITALIC 11 ON 14

AENEAN SAPIEN ODIO, dictum id, blandit non, nonummy eget, velit. Quisque id pede. Sed posuere tempor turpis. Curabitur fermentum, arcu vitae laoreet dignissim, lectus est conse- ***quat wisi, at molestie lorem leo sed pede. Pellentesque at lacus id mauris iaculis consequat. Mauris eu nulla vel eros faucibus ac-***

SHAKER EXTRABOLD CONDENSED & ITALIC 11 ON 14

PROIN SEMPER FACILISIS nibh. In diam tortor, facilisis a, posuere et, consequat nec, mi. Nunc pharetra orci eget est. Donec wisi. Suspendisse velit dui, consequat ac, dapibus ***vitae, hendrerit eu, felis. Ut at nisl et mauris pretium suscipit. Quisque et nunc ut justo convallis lacinia. Proin sodales eros ac***

SHAKER HEAVY CONDENSED & ITALIC 11 ON 14

SUSPENDISSE FAUCIBUS. PHASELLUS quis augue. Integer sed libero vel massa consequat eleifend. Quisque tincidunt est quis lectus. Duis posuere, elit at bibendum ***tincidunt, mauris turpis nonummy mi, eget semper tellus dolor at turpis. Pellentesque habitant morbi tristique senec-***

Shaker Regular

SHAKER LIGHT & ITALIC 11 ON 14

NULLA FACILISI. PELLENTESQUE habitant morbi tristique senectus et netus et malesuada fames ac turpis egestas. Proin venenatis, magna ac egestas euismod, eros turpis dapibus urna, nec blandit *ligula nisl in leo. Nam nonummy vestibulum tellus. Cras a mi quis nulla sagittis semper. Nullam tincidunt laoreet metus. Phasellus*

SHAKER REGULAR & ITALIC 11 ON 14

SUSPENDISSE FEUGIAT PRETIUM justo. Nunc sagittis arcu eget nulla. Etiam ac felis. In rutrum, libero eget convallis blandit, justo nibh faucibus ligula, quis dictum eros *arcu sit amet mauris. Nulla consectetuer est ut erat. Nullam dignissim adipiscing risus. Etiam bibendum elementum*

SHAKER BOLD & ITALIC 11 ON 14

VIVAMUS VULPUTATE LECTUS a nulla. Aliquam ut mi. Praesent sed libero at diam bibendum convallis. Sed elementum viverra velit. Quisque erat neque, rutrum ut, tincidunt non, ***vestibulum non, eros. Nunc convallis turpis nec augue. Fusce iaculis tempus mi. Etiam sodales. Aliquam elit ipsum, egestas***

SHAKER EXTRABOLD & ITALIC 11 ON 14

QUISQUE DOLOR QUAM, PRETIUM at, lacinia vel, varius at, odio. Curabitur mollis risus eget libero. Nullam nec dui in odio faucibus accumsan. Donec dictum vulputate ante. ***Pellentesque fringilla risus mollis lacus. Nullam vestibulum nibh non wisi. Donec lobortis faucibus mauris.***

SHAKER HEAVY & ITALIC 11 ON 14

MORBI PULVINAR, DOLOR in tempor aliquam, augue wisi placerat velit, vitae egestas purus lacus vel quam. Integer wisi. Praesent nec ante. Quisque porttitor ***imperdiet augue. Fusce placerat pharetra velit. Ut lectus orci, cursus sed, tempus vel, condimentum a, lacus.***

Shaker Wide

SHAKER LIGHT WIDE & ITALIC 11 ON 14

NULLA LACINIA URNA NEC SEM. In eget velit in turpis sagittis varius. Vivamus quis orci. Lorem ipsum dolor sit amet, consectetuer adipiscing elit. Donec eget elit. *Morbi justo. Duis nec sem in est porttitor pharetra. Curabitur quis nunc. Aliquam libero. Etiam dapibus nonummy*

SHAKER WIDE & ITALIC 11 ON 14

SUSPENDISSE POTENTI. Quisque ut wisi sed massa euismod ullamcorper. Curabitur posuere, lorem et placerat vehicula, justo purus blandit massa, et venenatis *massa lorem sed lectus. Nulla ut justo. Vivamus iaculis pharetra neque. In rhoncus justo eu nisl. Cras euismod*

SHAKER BOLD WIDE & ITALIC 11 ON 14

DUIS BLANDIT, DOLOR bibendum adipiscing suscipit, arcu augue faucibus nulla, dictum rhoncus turpis justo id odio. Sed consequat mi eu neque. Pellen***tesque elit libero, elementum semper, commodo at, mollis id, libero. Fusce laoreet neque et elit. Fusce lacus***

SHAKER EXTRABOLD WIDE & ITALIC 11 ON 14

DONEC LACUS. CRAS euismod tellus sit amet justo. Maecenas erat leo, volutpat ac, eleifend ac, porttitor non, ante. Suspendisse placerat nulla vitae ***neque. Vestibulum odio metus, venenatis ut, ornare eu, commodo at, sem. Fusce neque. Suspendisse***

SHAKER HEAVY WIDE & ITALIC 11 ON 14

ETIAM QUIS FELIS NEC tortor lacinia tristique. Vestibulum imperdiet. Pellentesque euismod. Cras vel mi vitae velit dapibus vulputate. Nul***lam dictum ornare justo. Cras faucibus dictum eros. Nulla vestibulum blandit eros. Praesent***

DAVID MALJKOVIĆ

Born 1973, lives and works in Zagreb and Berlin

SELECTED SOLO EXHIBITIONS:

2007 P.S.1 Contemporary Art Center
NEW YORK • USA

Whitechapel Art Gallery
LONDON • UNITED KINGDOM

52nd *Venice Biennale,* Croatian Pavillion
VENICE • ITALY

2006 *These Days* [with **Yael Bartana**]
Gallery Nova
ZAGREB • CROATIA

2005 *Scene for New Heritage*
Van Abbemuseum
EINDHOVEN • NETHERLANDS

SELECTED GROUP EXHIBITIONS:

2007 *Magellanic Cloud*
Centre Pompidou
PARIS • FRANCE

Elephant Cemetery
Artist Space
NEW YORK • USA

2006 *Art, Life & Confusion, 47th October Art Salon*
BELGRADE • SERBIA

Interrupted Histories
The Museum of Modern Art
LJUBLJANA • SLOVENIA

2005 *Go Inside, Tirana Biennale 3*
TIRANA • ALBANIA

9th International İstanbul Biennial
ISTANBUL • TURKEY

Example in Shaker, typography Dejan Kršić from *Ground Lost, Graz/Zagreb,* 2007

the shire types

MAIN FORMS

AAaaaaBBCCCCDDEEEEeFFFFf
GGggHHIIiiiiJJJjjKKKKLLLLLLM
MmmmmmNNnnnnOPPQQQRR
rrrrSTTtttUUUUUUUVVVVWWW
WWWXXXXYYYYYYYZZZZÀÁÂÃÄĀ
ĂÅǺĄÀÁÂÃÄĀĂÅǺĄàáâãäāăåǻąàáâ
ãäāăåǻąàáâãäāăåǻąàáâãäāăåǻą
ÆÆÆÆŒǼǼǽǽǿĆĈČĊÇĆĈČĊÇćĉč
ċçćĉčċçćĉčċçĎĎĐĐÈÉÊĚËĒĔĖĘÈÉÊĚË
ĒĔĖĘèéêěëēĕėęèéêěëēĕėęèéêěëēĕėę
ĜĞĠĢĜĞĠĢĝğġģĝğġģĤĤĦĦÌÍÎĨÏĪĬĮİÌÍÎ
ĨÏĪĬĮìíîĩïīĭįıìíîĩïīĭįıìíîĩïīĭįıìíîĩïīĭ
įıIJIJijijijijĴĴĵĵĵĵĶĶķķĹĽĻŁĿĹĽĻŁĿ
ĺľļłŀĺľļłŀĺľļłŀĺľļłŀŃŇÑŅŃŇÑŅńňñ
ņńňñņńňñņòóôõöōŏőØøŒ
ŒŒŒŒŔŘŖŔŘŖŕřŗŕřŗŕřŗŕřŗŚŜŠŞŞ
ŞßßßßŤŢŦŤŢŦťţŧťţŧťţŧťţŧÙÚÛŨÜŪ
ŬŮŰŲÙÚÛŨÜŪŬŮŰŲùúûũüūŭůűųùú
ûũüūŭůűųùúûũüūŭůűųùúûũüūŭ
ůűųẀẂŴẄẀẂŴẄẁẃŵẅẁẃŵẅẁẃ
ŵẅẁẃŵẅỲÝŶŸỲÝŶŸỳýŷÿỳýŷÿỳýŷ
ÿỳýŷÿŹŽŻŹŽŻŹŽŻŹŽŻŊŊŋŋŋÞþ

LIGATURES

fi fi fi fi fi fi fl fl fl fl fl fl

FIGURES, CURRENCY & RELATED FORMS

011112222334455566667777899

€$¢£££££ƒ¥¹²³ ½¼¾

+−±×÷=≠≈~^<>≤≥¬◊|¦∞∂∫√ΔΩΠΣπ

µµµµµµ/%‰№№℮¤ℓ°ªªªªªº

PUNCTUATION & MARKS

'"‘’“”‚„‹›«»‚„'"‘’“”‚„'"‘’“”‚„

‹›«».,;;::.;;::......-·

!¡!¡!¡!¡?¿?¿?¿

&&&()[]{}\/**†‡§¶•#_-–—

ⒶⓐⓐⒸⓅⓇ™™™™™™™

ARROWS

←↑→↓↖↗↘↙

ACCENTS

`´ˆˇ˜¨¯˘˚˝˙ˈ

¸˛''''

The Shire Types™ consist of six fonts in one weight
Cheshire, Shropshire, Derbyshire, Staffordshire, Warwickshire, Worcestershire

random
oui
PALIGĀ!
go
NORTHWEST
takk

não

LINJEBUSSEN

BANNAÐ

Köln

ENLIGHTENMENT

Ei!

Wayfarer Regular

CAPITALS

ABCDEFGHIJKLMNOPQRSTUVWXYZ
ÀÁÂÃÄĀĂÅǺĄÆǼĆĈČĊÇĎĐÈÉÊĚËĒ
ĔĖĘĜĞĠĢĤĦÌÍÎĨÏĪĬİĮIJĴĶĹĽĻŁĿŃŇÑŅ
ÒÓÔÕÖŌŎŐØǾŒŔŘŖŚŜŠŞȘŤŢŦÙÚÛ
ŨÜŪŬŮŰŲẀẂŴẄỲÝŶŸŹŽŻŊĐÞ

LOWERCASE

abcdefghijklmnopqrstuvwxyz
àáâãäāăåǻąæǽćĉčċçďđèéêěëēĕėęĝğġģ
ĥħìíîĩïīĭįıijĵķĺľļłŀńňñņòóôõöōŏőøǿœŕřŗ
śŝšşșßťţŧùúûũüūŭůűųẁẃŵẅỳýŷÿźžżŋðþ

SMALL CAPITALS

ABCDEFGHIJKLMNOPQRSTUVWXYZ
ÀÁÂÃÄĀĂÅǺĄÆǼĆĈČĊÇĎĐÈÉÊĚËĒĔĖĘ
ĜĞĠĢĤĦÌÍÎĨÏĪĬİĮIJĴĶĹĽĻŁĿŃŇÑŅ
ÒÓÔÕÖŌŎŐØǾŒŔŘŖŚŜŠŞȘŤŢŦ
ÙÚÛŨÜŪŬŮŰŲẀẂŴẄỲÝŶŸŹŽŻŊĐÞ

LIGATURES

fb ffb ff fh ffh fi ffi fj ffj fk ffk fl ffl fþ

Wayfarer Italic

CAPITALS

ABCDEFGHIJKLMNOPQRSTUVWXYZ
ÀÁÂÃÄĀĂÅǺĄÆǼĆĈČĊÇĎĐÈÉÊĚËĒ
ĔĖĘĜĞĠĢĤĦÌÍÎĨÏĪĬİĮĲĴĶĹĽĻŁĿŃŇÑŅ
ÒÓÔÕÖŌŎŐØǾŒŔŘŖŚŜŠŞȘŤŢŦÙÚÛ
ŨÜŪŬŮŰŲẀẂŴẄỲÝŶŸŹŽŻŊÐÞ

LOWERCASE

abcdefghijklmnopqrstuvwxyz
àáâãäāăåǻąæǽćĉčċçďđèéêěëēĕėęĝğġģ
ĥħìíîĩïīĭįıĳĵķĺľļłŀńňñņòóôõöōŏőøǿœŕřŗ
śŝšşșßťţŧùúûũüūŭůűųẁẃŵẅỳýŷÿźžżŋðþ

SMALL CAPITALS

ABCDEFGHIJKLMNOPQRSTUVWXYZ
ÀÁÂÃÄĀĂÅǺĄÆǼĆĈČĊÇĎĐÈÉÊĚËĒĔĖĘ
ĜĞĠĢĤĦÌÍÎĨÏĪĬİĮĲĴĶĹĽĻŁĿŃŇÑŅ
ÒÓÔÕÖŌŎŐØǾŒŔŘŖŚŜŠŞȘŤŢŦ
ÙÚÛŨÜŪŬŮŰŲẀẂŴẄỲÝŶŸŹŽŻŊÐÞ

LIGATURES

fb ffb ff fh ffh fi ffi fj ffj fk ffk fl ffl fþ

Wayfarer™ has six weights plus italics
Light, Regular, Medium, SemiBold, Bold, Heavy

Wayfarer Regular

SUPERIORS

abcdefghijklmnopqrstuvwxyz

ABCDEFGHIJKLMNOPQRSTUVWXYZ

FIGURES, CURRENCY & RELATED FORMS

[DEFAULT] 0123456789€$¢£ƒ¥

[TABULAR] 0123456789€$£¥

[OLDSTYLE] 0123456789€$£¥

[TABULAR] 0123456789€$£¥

[SMALL CAPITAL] 0123456789€$£¥

[SUPERIOR] 0123456789+−=() [INFERIOR] 0123456789+−=()

[NUMERATOR] 0123456789+−=() [DENOMINATOR] 0123456789+−=()

½ ⅓ ⅔ ¼ ¾ ⅕ ⅖ ⅗ ⅘ ⅙ ⅚ ⅛ ⅜ ⅝ ⅞

$\frac{1}{2}\frac{1}{3}\frac{2}{3}\frac{1}{4}\frac{3}{4}\frac{1}{5}\frac{2}{5}\frac{3}{5}\frac{4}{5}\frac{1}{6}\frac{5}{6}\frac{1}{8}\frac{3}{8}\frac{5}{8}\frac{7}{8}$

+−±×÷=≠≈~^<>≤≥¬◊|¦∞∂∫√∆Ω∏∑µπ

/ % ‰ № ℮ ¤ ℓ ° ª º

PUNCTUATION & MARKS

' " ‘ ’ ‘ ’ “ ” “ ” ‚ „ ‹ › ‹ › « » « » . , : ; … · ! ¡ ¡ ! ¡ ? ¿ ¿ ? ¿

&&()()()[][][]{}{}{}\/*†‡§¶•#_-‐–—―

@@@©©℗℗®™

ARROWS

← ↑ → ↓ ↖ ↗ ↘ ↙ ← ↑ → ↓ ↖ ↗ ↘ ↙

ACCENTS

` ` ´ ´ ˆ ˆ ˇ ˇ ˜ ˜ ¨ ¨ ¯ ¯ ˘ ˘ ˚ ˚ ˝ ˝ ˙ ˙

¸ ˛ ,

Wayfarer Italic

SUPERIORS

abcdefghijklmnopqrstuvwxyz

ABCDEFGHIJKLMNOPQRSTUVWXYZ

FIGURES, CURRENCY & RELATED FORMS

[DEFAULT] *0123456789€$¢£ƒ¥*

[TABULAR] *0123456789€$£¥*

[OLDSTYLE] *0123456789€$£¥*

[TABULAR] *0123456789€$£¥*

[SMALL CAPITAL] *0123456789€$£¥*

[SUPERIOR] *0123456789+−=()* [INFERIOR] *0123456789+−=()*

[NUMERATOR] *0123456789+−=()* [DENOMINATOR] *0123456789+−=()*

½ ⅓ ⅔ ¼ ¾ ⅕ ⅖ ⅗ ⅘ ⅙ ⅚ ⅛ ⅜ ⅝ ⅞

1/2 1/3 2/3 1/4 3/4 1/5 2/5 3/5 4/5 1/6 5/6 1/8 3/8 5/8 7/8

+−±×÷=≠≈~^<>≤≥¬◊|¦∞∂∫√ΔΩΠΣµπ

/ % ‰ № ℮ ¤ ℓ ° ª º

PUNCTUATION & MARKS

'"‘’‚‛“”„‟„ ‹›‹›«»«» .,:;... ·!¡!¡?¿?¿

&&()()()[][][]{}{}{}{}\/†‡§¶•#_-‐–−—―*

@@@©©℗℗®™

ARROWS

← ↑ → ↓ ↖ ↗ ↘ ↙ ← ↑ → ↓ ↖ ↗ ↘ ↙

ACCENTS

` ` ´ ´ ^ ^ ˇ ˇ ˜ ˜ ¨ ¨ ¯ ¯ ˘ ˘ ˚ ˚ ˝ ˝ ˙ ˙

¸ ˛ ,

Wayfarer was originally designed as the typeface for a new city centre wayfinding system for the city of Sheffield, UK.[1] It had been thought an existing type, Granby Condensed, would be suitable. The Granby family of types were developed during the 1930s as Stephenson Blake's contribution to the general cashing in of other foundries on the popularity of Monotype's Gill Sans and the geometric sans serifs being introduced by the continental type foundries. Many of the detailing features found in Granby link it closely to other types of that period. The most obvious influence is that of the London Underground typeface.[2] This is not surprising as Stephenson Blake were involved in the production of the Johnston wood letter used by London Underground.

Stephenson Blake's Granby

The London Underground type

Application of the original Granby Condensed type was, however, difficult practically. It was not available in digital form, and felt to be just too condensed, with the proportion of ascender to x-height, too uncomfortable for use on the signing project. So there arose an opportunity to design a new typeface and at the same time tailor it to the specific needs of the Sheffield signs. A new type could address the formal requirements of a signing context, while retaining the characteristic diamond dot of the Granby faces.

Left: Granby Condensed
Right: Grotesque № 8

It was also possible to widen the typographic references for the new type. I was keen to look at other early sans serif letterforms, especially those from Stephenson Blake and most notably their Grotesque series.[3] These most idiosyncratic of designs are full of warmth, have an informal rhythm and a vitality to their shapes, all of which help create interesting word patterns. These types fell out of favour as designers looked to the cleaner and more standardised forms of later interpretations of the idea of the grotesque type. The Swiss School in particular did much to launch such 'neo-grotesque' types into the ubiquity of use they still enjoy today, offering a more functional image and an extended range of integrated weights and styles.

The lowercase letters of Wayfarer incorporate a variety of terminal endings. These help reflect the informal quality found in the Grotesque types

The rhythm of Wayfarer is similar to that of Granby, but is combined with an approach to character detailing which echoes the informal variety found in the Grotesques. The character set covers most languages that use the Latin letter and includes many useful extras such as small capitals, arrows, superiors and fractions. As a feature of Wayfarer, superior small capitals have been included. Examples of their use can typically be found in contractions on older street name lettering and in some business names.

Street = ST
Road = RD
Sons = SONS
Brothers = BROS

Superior small capitals in use

1. Information about the design company Atelier Works that commissioned the original type can be found at www.atelierworks.co.uk
2. The London Underground typeface was designed in 1916 by Edward Johnston
3. A large family of types based on nineteenth-century models

WAYFARER LIGHT 9 ON 12

PROIN QUIS NULLA AT VELIT facilisis dignissim. Suspendisse nonummy purus quis lorem. Vivamus eu dolor id ullamcorper sollicitudin. Cras rutrum lacinia erat. Mauris neque sapien, venenatis ut, condimentum ut, venenatis vel, metus. *Morbi ac ligula. Proin quis ante vel sapien volutpat ornare. Nulla rhoncus condimentum nibh. Pellentesque sed mi. Morbi lobortis, urna mattis vestibulum*

WAYFARER REGULAR 9 ON 12

ETIAM METUS. VESTIBULUM NEQUE ODIO, consequat eu, vestibulum ut, ornare hendrerit, odio. Cras viverra mi sed nisl. Class aptent taciti sociosqu ad litora torquent per conubia nostra, per inceptos hymenaeos. In hac habitasse platea *dictumst. Suspendisse eget ipsum et neque ultrices tristique. Aliquam in sem ut lacus accumsan porttitor. Vivamus non tellus. Etiam eu lectus. Maecenas wisi*

WAYFARER MEDIUM 9 ON 12

MAURIS SEMPER, QUAM SED LAOREET dapibus, lorem velit ultricies nibh, in venenatis urna lorem a lorem. Nullam ornare faucibus dui. Sed porttitor augue. Phasellus vestibulum, ligula a varius pharetra, justo velit pretium lacus, id *fermentum lacus pede non purus. Etiam ac lacus at ante sollicitudin sollicitudin. Quisque urna. Suspendisse est. Vivamus in est sed nulla consectetuer pretium.*

WAYFARER SEMIBOLD 9 ON 12

VESTIBULUM VEL URNA. ALIQUAM ERAT volutpat. Sed nec urna non lorem eleifend eleifend. Pellentesque habitant morbi tristique senectus et netus et malesuada fames ac turpis egestas. Proin ac mauris. Cras augue. Vestibulum ***ante ipsum primis in faucibus orci luctus et ultrices posuere cubilia Curae; Maecenas ultricies justo vulputate eros. Sed sed leo dignissim lectus***

WAYFARER BOLD 9 ON 12

ETIAM QUIS FELIS NEC TORTOR lacinia tristique. Vestibulum imperdiet. Pellentesque euismod. Cras vel mi vitae velit dapibus vulputate. Nullam dictum ornare justo. Cras faucibus dictum eros. Nulla vestibulum blandit eros. ***Praesent scelerisque. Morbi vitae wisi. In ultrices nulla eleifend turpis. Nulla sit amet est. Etiam ut wisi. Duis suscipit urna et metus. Pellentesque mi.***

WAYFARER HEAVY 9 ON 12

PELLENTESQUE PRETIUM TELLUS NON orci tincidunt luctus. Nulla facilisi. Aenean rutrum nisl sed turpis. Nulla diam magna, ultrices gravida, hendrerit vitae, elementum ac, sem. In mauris pede, hendrerit et, malesuada et, ***vestibulum vel, mauris. Curabitur luctus velit. Phasellus eleifend, justo vel iaculis facilisis, nibh lacus ornare lorem, ac lacinia est urna fermentum enim.***

A 1
(Worksop 9)
Doncaster 22
(Sheffield 26)

A 1
(Worksop 9)
Doncaster 22
(Sheffield 26)

WAYFARER LIGHT 12 ON 15

DONEC LACUS. CRAS EUISMOD tellus sit amet justo. Maecenas erat leo, volutpat ac, eleifend ac, porttitor non, ante. *Suspendisse placerat nulla vitae neque. Vestibulum odio metus, venenatis ut, ornare eu, commodo at, sem. Fusce*

WAYFARER REGULAR 12 ON 15

DUIS BLANDIT, DOLOR BIBENDUM adipiscing suscipit, arcu augue faucibus nulla, dictum rhoncus turpis justo id odio. *Sed consequat mi eu neque. Pellentesque elit libero, elementum semper, commodo at, mollis id, libero. Fusce*

WAYFARER MEDIUM 12 ON 15

DONEC FEUGIAT ENIM NON quam. Vestibulum ac felis sed elit pulvinar scelerisque. Suspendisse luctus euismod dolor. *Nam non neque. Cras eget urna vel eros semper tincidunt. Suspendisse potenti. In purus. Sed id velit vel diam tempor*

WAYFARER SEMIBOLD 12 ON 15

PELLENTESQUE PORTTITOR SAGITTIS nisl. Fusce dictum, justo ac adipiscing congue, mi est convallis leo, quis auctor ***magna sapien sagittis sapien. Fusce arcu tortor, mattis quis, tincidunt nec, tristique id, enim. Aenean fermentum***

WAYFARER BOLD 12 ON 15

SUSPENDISSE POTENTI. QUISQUE ut wisi sed massa euismod ullamcorper. Curabitur posuere, lorem et ***placerat vehicula, justo purus blandit massa, et venenatis massa lorem sed lectus. Nulla ut justo. Vivamus iaculis***

WAYFARER HEAVY 12 ON 15

NULLA LACINIA URNA NEC SEM. In eget velit in turpis sagittis varius. Vivamus quis orci. Lorem ipsum dolor sit ***amet, consectetuer adipiscing elit. Donec eget elit. Morbi justo. Duis nec sem in est porttitor pharetra. Curabitur***

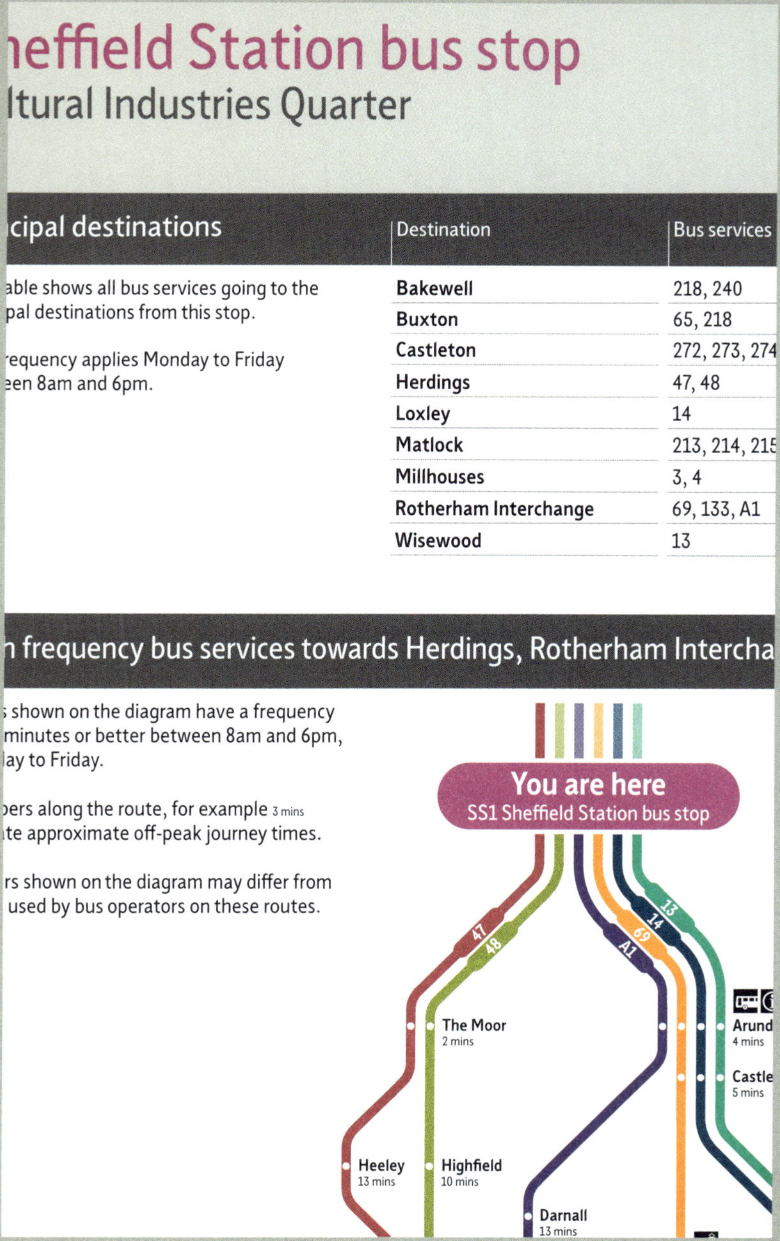

Example in Wayfarer, detail of sign design by City ID (www.cityid.co.uk)

THE ROUTE MASTER

Peak District National Park

London Rd

travel from A to B via C

Guide

Junction 5

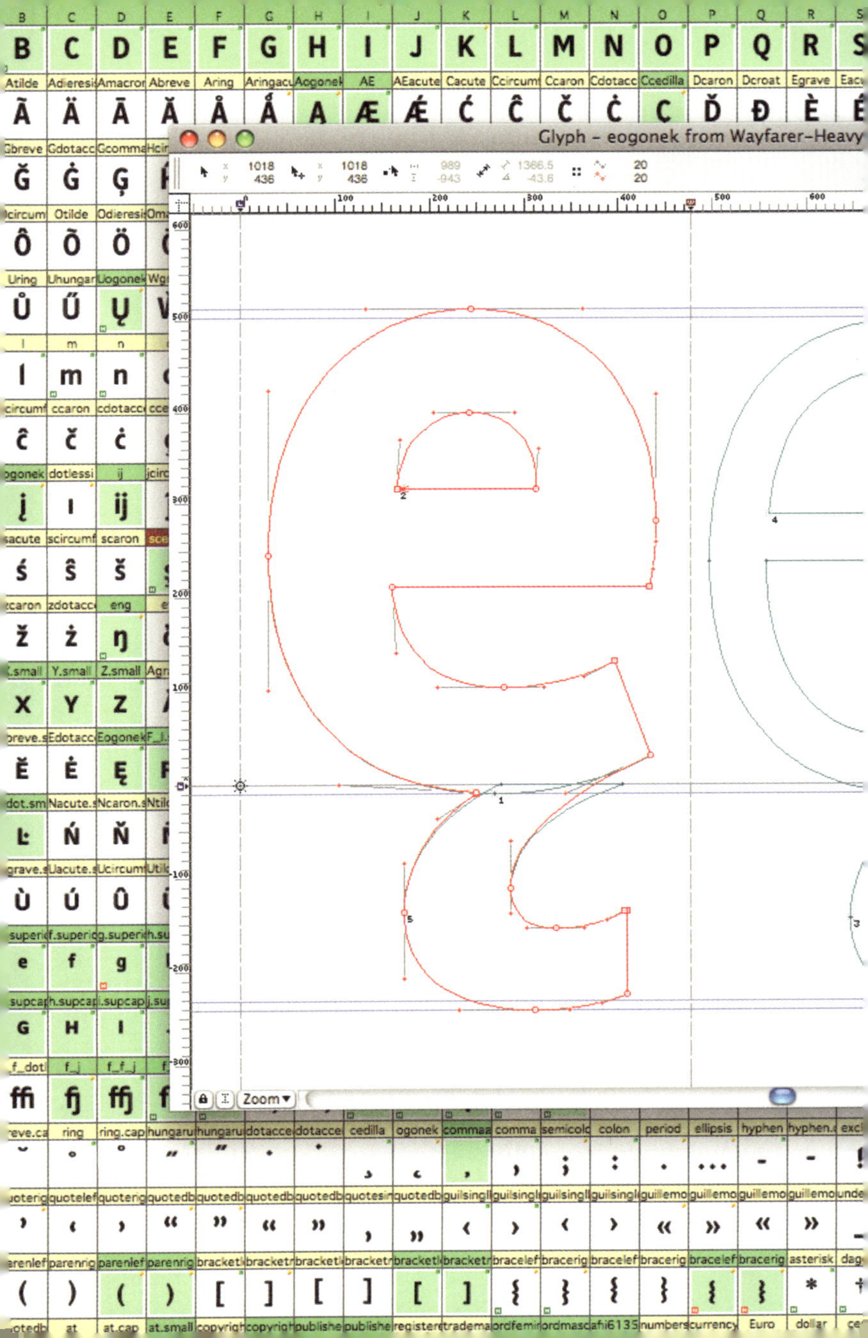

Glyph – eogonek from Wayfarer–Heavy
Atilde Adieresis Amacron Abreve Aring Aringacute Aogonek AE AEacute Cacute Ccircumflex Ccaron Cdotaccent Ccedilla Dcaron Dcroat Egrave
cedilla ogonek commaaccent comma semicolon colon period ellipsis hyphen
Zoom

For Brian Tankard

Published by Jeremy Tankard Typography Ltd, Cambridge 2008

Book designed and typeset by Jeremy Tankard using Adobe InDesign CS3
Printed in the United Kingdom by The Cloister Press, Cambridge

ISBN 0-9547736-1-6

www.typography.net

C	D	E	F	G	H	I	J	K	L	M	N	O	P	Q	R	S
Edieresis	Emacron	Ebreve	Edotacc	Eogonek	F_I.cap	F_L.cap	Gcircum	Gbreve	Gdotacc	Gcomma	Hcircum	Hbar	Igrave	Iacute	Icircumf	Itilde
Ë	Ē	Ĕ	Ė	Ę	FI	FL	Ĝ	Ğ	Ġ	Ģ	Ĥ	Ħ	Ì	Í	Î	Ĩ
Rcomma	Sacute	Scircumf	Scaron	Scedilla	Scomma	S_S.cap	Tcaron	Tcomma	Tbar	Ugrave	Uacute	Ucircumf	Utilde	Udieresis	Umacron	Ubreve
Ŗ	Ś	Ŝ	Š	Ş	Ș	SS	Ť	Ţ	Ŧ	Ù	Ú	Û	Ũ	Ü	Ū	Ŭ
n	o	p	q	r	s	t	u	v	w	x	y	z	agrave	aacute	acircumf	atilde
n	o	p	q	r	s	t	u	v	w	x	y	z	à	á	â	ã
igrave	iacute	icircumfl	itilde	idieresis	imacron	ibreve	iogonek	dotlessi	ij	jcircumfl	kcomma	lacute	lcaron	lcommaa	lslash	ldot
ì	í	î	ĩ	ï	ī	ĭ	į	ı	ĳ	ĵ	ķ	ĺ	ľ	ļ	ł	ŀ
utilde	udieresis	umacron	ubreve	uring	uhungar	uogonek	wgrave	wacute	wcircum	wdieresi	ygrave	yacute	ycircumf	ydieresis	zacute	zcaron
ũ	ü	ū	ŭ	ů	ű	ų	ẁ	ẃ	ŵ	ẅ	ỳ	ý	ŷ	ÿ	ź	ž
Agrave.s	Aacute.s	Acircum	Atilde.sn	Adieresis	Amacron	Abreve.s	Aring.sm	Aringacu	Aogonek	AE.small	AEacute	Cacute.s	Ccircum	Ccaron.s	Cdotacc	Ccedilla.
À	Á	Â	Ã	Ä	Ā	Ă	Å	Ǻ	Ą	Æ	Ǽ	Ć	Ĉ	Č	Ċ	Ç
Jcircumf	Kcomma	Lacute.s	Lcaron.s	Lcomma	Lslash.s	Ldot.sm	Nacute.s	Ncaron.s	Ntilde.sn	Ncomma	Ograve.s	Oacute.s	Ocircum	Otilde.sn	Odieresis	Omacron
Ĵ	Ķ	Ĺ	Ľ	Ļ	Ł	Ŀ	Ń	Ň	Ñ	Ņ	Ò	Ó	Ô	Õ	Ö	Ō
Wdieres	Ygrave.s	Yacute.s	Ycircumf	Ydieresis	Zacute.s	Zcaron.s	Zdotacc	Eng.sma	Eth.smal	Thorn.sn	a.superio	b.superio	c.superio	d.superio	e.superio	f.superio
Ẅ	Ỳ	Ý	Ŷ	Ÿ	Ź	Ž	Ż	Ŋ	Ð	Þ	a	b	c	d	e	f
Lambda	Mu	Nu	Xi	Omicron	Pi	Rho	Sigma	Tau	Upsilon	Phi	Chi	Psi	uni03A9	Alphaton	Epsilonto	Etatonos
Λ	Μ	Ν	Ξ	Ο	Π	Ρ	Σ	Τ	Υ	Φ	Χ	Ψ	Ω	Ά	Έ	Ή
pi	rho	sigma	sigmafin	tau	upsilon	phi	phi.alt	chi	psi	omega	alphaton	epsilont	etatonos	iotatono	iotadiere	iotadiere
π	ρ	σ	ς	τ	υ	φ	ϕ	χ	ψ	ω	ά	έ	ή	ί	ϊ	ΐ
Epsilont	Etatonos	Iotatono	Iotadiere	Iotadiere	Omicron	Upsilont	Upsilond	Upsilond	Omegat	Alphaton	Epsilont	Etatonos	Iotatono	Iotadiere	Omicron	Upsilont
Ε	Η	Ι	Ϊ	Ϊ	Ο	Υ	Ϋ	Ϋ	Ω	Ά	Έ	Ή	Ί	Ϊ	Ό	Ύ
afii1003	afii1003	afii1003	afii1003	afii1004	afii1004	afii1004	afii1004	afii1004	afii1004	afii1004	afii1004	afii1004	afii1004	afii1005	afii1005	afii1005
Т	У	Ф	Х	Ц	Ч	Ш	Щ	Ъ	Ы	Ь	Э	Ю	Я	Ѓ	Ґ	Ђ
afii1007	afii1008	afii1008	afii1008	afii1008	afii1008	afii1008	afii1008	afii1008	afii1008	afii1008	afii1009	afii1009	afii1009	afii1009	afii1009	afii1009
н	о	п	р	с	т	у	ф	х	ц	ч	ш	щ	ъ	ы	ь	э
afii1002	afii1002	afii1002	afii1002	afii1002	afii1002	afii1002	afii1002	afii1002	afii1003	afii1003	afii1003	afii1003	afii1003	afii1003	afii1003	afii1003
д	е	ё	ж	з	и	й	к	л	м	н	о	п	р	с	т	у
afii1014	fi	fl	ampersa	ampersa	breve.Cy	breve.Cy	grave	grave.ca	acute	acute.ca	circumfl	circumfle	caron	caron.ca	uni0315	tilde
ѵ	fi	fl	&	&	˘	˘	`	`	´	´	^	^	ˇ	ˇ	'	~
question	question	question	quotelef	quoterig	quotelef	quoterig	quotedb	quotedb	quotedb	quotedb	quotesin	quotedb	guilsingl	guilsingl	guilsingl	guilsingl
¿	?	¿	'	'	'	'	"	"	"	"	,	„	‹	›	‹	›
bracerig	asterisk	dagger	daggerd	section	paragrap	bar	brokenb	slash	backslas	asciicirc	asciitilde	quotesin	quotedb	at	at.cap	at.small
}	*	†	‡	§	¶	|	¦	/	\	^	~	'	"	@	@	@
yen.OT	zero.OT	one.OT	two.OT	three.OT	four.OT	five.OT	six.OT	seven.O	eight.OT	nine.OT	Euro.LT	dollar.LT	sterling.	yen.LT	zero.LT	one.LT
¥	0	1	2	3	4	5	6	7	8	9	€	$	£	¥	0	1
four.sma	five.sma	six.small	seven.sn	eight.sm	nine.sma	zerosup	onesupe	twosupe	threesup	foursupe	fivesupe	sixsuper	sevensu	eightsup	ninesupe	plussupe
4	5	6	7	8	9	0	1	2	3	4	5	6	7	8	9	+
minus.d	equal.d	parenlef	parenrig	zero.nur	one.num	two.num	three.nu	four.num	five.num	six.num	seven.n	eight.nu	nine.num	plus.nun	minus.n	equal.nu
				0	1	2	3	4	5	6	7	8	9	+	−	=